BREAKING BAD HABITS WITH MENTAL TOUGHNESS

THE ULTIMATE BLUEPRINT TO UNLOCK YOUR POTENTIAL WITH SELF DISCIPLINE HABITS THAT WILL LAST FOREVER (BUILDING WILLPOWER, SELF CONTROL, GOOD HABITS)

EDRIC SCHUMAN

SPECIAL BONUS!

Want This Bonus for Free?

Get FREE, unlimiited access to it and all of my new books by joining the Fan Base!

Scan with your camera to join!

CONTENTS

FATHER KNOWS BEST: HABITS MAKE A MAN

"We are what we repeatedly do. Excellence, then, is not an act, but a habit."

— ARISTOTLE

I grew up in the average American household. My parents studied in good schools and grew up to become upstanding citizens. They had the same hopes for my siblings and me. Somewhere along the way, I fell adrift. I grew up watching my father run every second of his life by the clock. He'd wake up at five-thirty, make the bed, set the kettle to boil, laid out clothes to wear to work, and then woke the children up for school.

Just as his life ran on routines, he expected ours to as well. As I grew up, I developed resistance to these routines. I was at a place in life where rebellion felt natural. I began acting out in little ways. I would go to school without combing my hair or leave a day's homework unfinished. They didn't feel too "deviant" back in the day, but they represented "lawlessness" and coming of age to me. I thought that was the right way to exist.

I moved out of my home at twenty after clearing a job interview at a local sales firm. It wasn't much, but I felt liberated. I could wake up when I wanted, go to sleep when I wanted, and order take-out every day. What wasn't there to love about this life? And I'll be honest— the first six months were blissful. Who doesn't dream about waking up at nine and going to the office in old clothes with disheveled hair? Okay, not all of us—but back then, I did.

Until the day I didn't.

The absence of a routine was sure to trip me up sooner or later, and when my deeds caught up with my life-style, what resulted was a hotpot. After ten-minute delays, I began reaching my office over an hour late. I was always on a junk-food high. My mood was terrible, and I had zero desire to make social connections. When all this culminated smack dab into a scary afternoon in the hospital, I began making sense of the wisdom in my father's ways.

All of us would like the gift of acting according to free will. We think that we deserve to live life on our own terms without realizing that life is a total of influences from internal and external cues. Let's say I think the habit of smoking is incredible, and I want to do it to keep up with the other boys in class. It's hip, it makes me feel socially accepted, and I'm free to do it because it's my life. But wait, am I really exercising free will here? Or am I being subjected to the influence of my peers who think that "smoking is cool"?

The thing about habits is that all of us have them, whether we like to admit it or not. Each of our actions, from going to bed, waking up, brushing our teeth, and spending nights out, results from a routine activity that has become a habit without which life seemingly doesn't make sense. In a way, living a life of lawlessness is itself a habit.

The issue? When you develop a habit that does you no good because you think it's "happening," the habit eventually controls you. I felt this acutely when I tried to bring order into my life. It was painfully boring at times to wake up at seven, cook my meals, and save money for a hypothetical future. But somewhere, a switch had gone off, and I'd become convinced that if anything were to control me, it would be my higher sense of wellbeing.

I wanted to enjoy life. I wanted to live it free from the control of the patterns I'd formed and which had sent me spiraling into depression. In the end, I got there. The more I rediscovered my perspective, the more coordinated my life felt, and my life became more wholesome. I still have difficult days, but I know that I can always pick myself up and get back on track.

Why? Because my mind has trained my body to always think twice before I act. I'm not the only one.

In a survey of 233 Richie Riches (predominantly self-made millionaires), Tom Corley, an accountant, and financial planner found certain common traits that defined all of them. First, they read. Voraciously, and more for acquiring knowledge than anything else. They spend time on their health and well-being. Corley noted that 61% of the millionaires also practiced "dream-setting," via which they envisioned their future selves with all their dreams turned to reality and spent some time putting this to paper.

He writes about other habits like sleeping seven hours and checking in with mentors, but most importantly, they make their own goals and pursue them with relentless passion (Corley, 2019). What is this, if not freedom? If freedom is the will to choose and build a life worth living, would you choose one that destroys everything by the time you are forty? Or would you choose one that keeps you in the light, always learning, always in the pursuit of your higher self, and always enjoying the journey?

I can tell you right now, when I was in the throes of struggling with my old habits, I was never happy. I was constantly tired, angry, and frustrated. I spent a year wrestling with myself and why I kept doing the things I "supposedly wanted to do all my life" but felt so darn unhappy. That's when I realized the truth of what my father practiced in his daily life. We are creatures of habit. A cause determines every action we take. There is no "I do this because I want to." Our wanting something itself is subject to cues from the environment.

I'll illustrate. My friend, Aaron, is a man who swears by habits. He went through a period of intense struggle to get to a place of being truly happy with himself. He used to think that spending long nights partying was something he enjoyed. As he delved deeper, he found that it wasn't so much the result of his "own choice," but something that "others did for relaxation, so he felt he had to do it too." This was a cue from his environment that he'd picked up on, and when he changed it, he found peace. That doesn't mean that he stopped spending time outdoors at night altogether. He simply cut back from doing it every night to a few times a month.

In *"30 One-Sentence Stories From People Who Have Built Better Habits,"* the author of *Atomic Habits,* James Clear talks about the importance of building habits based on the people we wish to become, rather than the things we want to do (Clear, 2021). The term for this is identity-based habits, and it makes sense. Think about it for a second. If you had two choices between becoming the best version of yourself or changing a single habit in the short term, which one do you think would sustain you?

If you are altering a habit, let's hypothetically assume waking up too late in the morning, would you rather do it to become healthier, or because you have to study for an immediate exam? The problem is that too many of us choose the latter option. As soon as the exam ends, so does our motivation to carry through with the habit. The result is an inconsistency which is good for no one.

James Clear shared success stories in this particular article. In one such success story, Roland improved his eating habits by identity change. Roland says that he'd tried in the past, but it became natural once he decided that he wanted to be someone who ate healthily. He changed his aim from "I want to stop eating bad food immediately" to "I am someone who eats healthy and leads a healthy life."

The change here is in perspective. Not only did Roland approach his desire for change with positivity, but he also thought long-term. Giving up bad food can make you feel good for two days, but when the craving hits, it's a straight turn to McDonald's. I've been there. But when you change your long-term goal to "I want a healthy life," your perspective is altered. You're not thinking of things like "I can eat bad food one day and give up again tomorrow." You are thinking of being healthy every day.

And that's just the level of understanding I want you to develop. Together, through the time we spend reading this book, we will get there. You want to develop mental toughness and an accountability attitude so that you may become more self-reliant and better able to deal with difficult circumstances. But this can be difficult without the correct guidance. Which is why I'm here to help.

Making people aware of their inner strengths and coming to terms with their mental toughness is my life's biggest passion. There was a time when instant gratification almost destroyed every aspect of my life. Learning mental toughness and using it to train my mind to make choices came afterward, and I was alone for most of the journey.

You are not. I'm here for you. Break Bad Habits With Mental Toughness shows you how to improve your mental toughness and get rid of harmful habits for good. In addition, the book examines the seven important mental toughness abilities and how to develop them. This is a labor of love, and within it, I will share each and everything that I have learned in the journey to living my best life. As will you.

Are you ready to begin the journey? Welcome to the future of a brand new, more mature, happier, and healthier you.

Come. Let's begin.

1

AN OVERVIEW OF MENTAL TOUGHNESS

"Champions aren't made in the gyms. Champions are made from something they have deep inside them-

A desire, a dream, a vision."

— MUHAMMAD ALI

Years back, when I was just getting out of a rut of bad habits, I was handed a very ambitious project. It was everything I could have asked for, and the returns were enormous. But the work was equally tricky and tiring. Before I knew it, I was putting in sixty hours a week at work to get things prepped, making sheets, constantly brainstorming, and perennially on edge. A point came where it felt like nothing I was doing would be enough. I was on the verge of giving up. I called my mother one day, tired and out of my wits. I was about to give up on everything I had done and tell her I was returning home. She listened to me quietly while I ranted.

Once I had finished, she told me only one thing. *"Your father used to tell me that he'd like to retire someday when all of you settled down. I watched him work fifteen hours a day to make ends meet. I wondered how he had it in him, how he managed to bear so much, do so much. One night, he came home so late that we ended up fighting. I asked him why he was doing so much. He took one look at the little bedroom—for we were not wealthy enough to give you boys separate rooms at the time. And he told me that his mother had raised a warrior. 'A warrior can lose everything, but he always has the mental toughness to fall back on. I have my strength inside me every day.' Son, I raised you the same way."*

I never looked back. And neither will you.

I have a fundamental question. What does mental toughness mean to you? Going by the definition offered by *Mental Toughness, Inc.* (Duran, 2020), mental toughness is *"the ability to resist, manage and overcome doubts, worries, concerns and the circumstances that prevent you from succeeding."* I like to sum it up using a well-known quote—*when the going gets tough, the tough get going.*

What does this mean, though? How would you define the parameters of "being good at something"—and this can be anything. What makes a good parent, a good employee, a good boss, a good swimmer, or a good student? Why is it that when goals are set, some of us stick to them without fail, while others slip and veer off course?

UNDERSTANDING MENTAL TOUGHNESS

We tend to generalize successful people by their cognitive or physical skills—*"Oh, she always comes first because she's so brainy." "He's built to win. Have you seen that body?" "His parents are both so successful; it must be in the genes."* Do these generalizations sound familiar to you? We've all made them. But if you genuinely look at the little quirks that make successful people, you'll find that they have the persistent ability to weather any storm.

This is the lasting definition of success.

In fact, research suggests that intelligence, for instance, accounts for just about 30% of your overall achievements, that too at the very upper end. So your physical and genetic gifts may not play as significant a role as you'd think.

On the same lines, research is beginning to show that mental toughness plays a significant role in achieving the goals you set for yourself, be it in health, business, relationships, or life itself. While you can't change your genes or the things you are born with, you can certainly build mental toughness.

Now a professor at Pennsylvania University, Angela Duckworth began her professional life teaching math to seventh graders in NYC public schools. Around this time, she discovered that some of her best students weren't the smartest ones but the ones who worked round the clock. This realization propelled her career as a research psychologist to understand foundational traits like self-control, perseverance, and grit (mental toughness) and their roles in achievement.

She studied children and adults in exacting situations—from US West Point Military cadets to rookie teachers to contestants in national Spelling Bee competitions. In each case, she posed the same question to her participants—*who are successful here, and why so?*

Can you guess the answer? Across different situations, one main factor won as the profound predictor of what constitutes success—*grit*. Grit, or mental toughness, allowed the successful respondents to put in hard work and maintain focus, not for a definitive period, but *endlessly.* She made a grit scale featuring questions like

"I have overcome drawbacks to triumph over important challenges." Respondents had to mark themselves on a scale of one to five, with one measuring as *"not at all like me"* to five measuring as *"very much like me."* The grit score was calculated to determine how it could lead to success.

Duckworth used this scale in Chicago Public Schools to judge whether grit in junior year students could have something to do with graduation the following year. For the survey, students answered questions on the Grit Scale and other criteria that are recognized to influence graduation, such as safety in the classroom and support from teachers and peers as well as parental encouragement and conscientiousness.

Even after considering these and other predictors, such as grades and test scores, and demographics, Duckworth and her colleagues discovered that juniors with the greatest tenacity were more likely than their mentally fragile classmates to graduate from high school with flying colors.

Additionally, Duckworth discovered some other defining factors of students who demonstrated grit:

- Undergraduate Ivy League students with more grit accumulated higher GPAs than their peers, even with lower SAT scores in some instances.

- Comparisons between two same-aged individuals with differing levels of education revealed that grit and not intelligence is the more accurate predictor of better education.
- In National Spelling Bee competitions, competitors who outperformed their peers did not do it because of higher IQ. Rather, they displayed immense commitment and grit to practice for the competition.

The conclusion was that grit is necessary for notable achievements in different professions, be it banking, painting, journalism, medicine, law, or academia. Grit or mental toughness is the defining characteristic of a star performer, and those with a sustained commitment to their goals and ambitions have therefore always awed others. This is why the tortoise wins the race, not the rabbit which can run faster.

Grit, my friend, is what will carry you through. Between someone who displays talent but is inherently lazy, and someone who is committed to success in the game, the committed player will always shine.

The measure of mental toughness is consistency. To illustrate, if you are a mentally tough athlete, it means that you work out more consistently, you eat right even on the days your body just wants soda and fries, and you keep your eyes ahead all the time. You don't miss assignments, and you know that loyalty trumps all.

To be a mentally tough leader, you have to show that you are committed and that you will achieve what you have set out to do. You establish a clear set of mini-goals that help you in the pursuit of the big one. You are not let down by short-term agendas, criticism, or hectic timelines because you know that the end you are working towards is more important than any small glitches along the way. And you don't just self-motivate. You push everyone around you to become the best versions of themselves. This is consistency.

Whether you are an employee, a boss, an artist, an entrepreneur, or a home-maker, every mentally tough human being delivers on a more consistent basis. I speak from experience when I say that in my personal life, the most successful family-makers are also those who run on a schedule, not at random intervals when the motivation strikes. To be mentally tough, you approach your daily routines based on priorities. You know what needs to be done first—and after a time, this knowledge comes naturally, from a subconscious level.

I know that this is easier said than done.

SO, WHY DO WE NEED MENTAL TOUGHNESS?

Many of us develop subconscious insecurities that stop us from becoming the best versions of ourselves. The problem happens when we fail to keep our insecurities aside and let them take control of our lives. When we do this, our performance becomes secondary to what we are capable of. The good thing is that mental toughness can't come overnight, it needs practice and training so that your perseverance overshadows your negative self-talk to make you someone who is inherently and consistently positive.

A little positive reinforcement can go a long way. If you are always entertaining negative thoughts like *"I'm not capable of this", "I'm not good enough for this",* and *"This is far too difficult for me,"* you are automatically reinforcing a negative thought pattern. The negative thought pattern will make you *internalize that you aren't good enough for anything.* When negative thoughts pervade your brain, the muscles of your body *actually react to this thought.*

Our negative thoughts can in turn impact your physical and mental performance. Focusing on positivity can be difficult because our bodies are hard-wired to look at dangers first, even when risks may not be present. When presented with prioritizing between good and evil, we always look at the evil things first. This was once necessary.

Our ancestors lived dangerous lives, constantly on the run and needing to defend themselves from dangers. Our negativity bias was born as a survival mechanism to protect our ancestors. It helped them perceive threats. But in the contemporary context, this bias has become counter-productive.

This negativity bias makes us spend too much time worrying about minor frustrations and ignore the things that we are capable of, including how gritty and mentally tough we can be. In other words, your attitude and belief about what you can accomplish are necessary *to help you achieve what you set out to. If you believe you can't do it, you can't—it's as simple as that.*

Let's break this down and look at seven key reasons why mental toughness is so essential to success.

FIRST, MENTAL TOUGHNESS HELPS YOU IN VANQUISHING SELF-DOUBT.

Regardless of what our ambitions are, all of us know how debilitating self-doubt can become at times. It takes control of our systems and makes us feel incapacitated even before we have done something significant. But, questioning your abilities to attain a goal is a natural part of the process of attaining the goal. When you develop mental toughness, you will be able to reframe negative self-talk patterns with awareness of how much you can do, and this will help you in working towards achieving your goal with renewed confidence.

Your awareness plays the most important role here. Taking a step back, seeing the direction you're moving in, and taking action against negative ideas and words is possible if you grasp the bleak reality they produce. It's possible to achieve this by using ideas and phrases that inspire optimism, confidence, bravery, and desire to counterattack.

Whether good or bad, the words you speak have an impact on your outlook and, as a result, the way things turn out for you. Always keep in mind that the instant you open your lips to speak, the wheels of creation begin to turn in earnest, and affect how you think and act. No matter what's bothering you, recognize the worry it symbolizes and take immediate action by verbally confronting those worries.

The next time you find yourself going down a rabbit hole of negative thinking, shake your head, run your hand across a pillow or a hard surface and tell yourself, *"I am present in this moment. I choose not to let irrational thoughts get the better of me."*

NEXT, MENTAL TOUGHNESS MOTIVATES YOU TO KEEP GOING.

Human motivation does not flow in one continuous thread. It can ebb and flow, and all of us have days when we feel exhausted and ones where we think we can take on the world. However, the most successful among us know that the problematic days never last just as much as the easy ones—the decisive factor is not about *getting* motivated, but in *staying motivated despite the circumstances.*

Mental toughness focuses on consistency and helps you move towards your goal irrespective of the hard days when all you want is a cup of hot chocolate and cuddles. It reminds you what you are capable of, that you are not a failure, and that the only roadblock in your way is your *own resistance to change.*

With mental toughness, you can dig deep and uncover the inner motivation that is always there and tap into it to overcome discouragement, lack of ambition, and exhaustion.

MENTAL TOUGHNESS IS AN EFFECTIVE SHIELD AGAINST DISCOURAGING ADVICE.

My mother used to tell me that since people have tongues, they will wag. And sometimes, the sounds they produce are only sounds—you don't have to pay attention to them.

This is not an easy thing to achieve, especially if you want to please someone else or you need to prove your worth to them. People's opinions can cast a shadow on your voice and beliefs.

With mental toughness, you will be able to turn your thoughts inward and focus on the one voice that counts —your own. The thought process will change from relying on others for appreciation to becoming the best version of yourself in your own eyes. After all, this is one life, and you have to live it. Nobody else will do the living for you. So, why not create something beautiful for yourself?

Being strong will keep you grounded and true to your values. Your focus will remain centered on making wise decisions that will cause better outcomes for *you*, regardless of what feedback the world around you has. Remember that with success, you draw envy. Rise above it.

MENTAL TOUGHNESS IS A SURE-FIRE WAY TO HELP YOU LEARN FROM YOUR MISTAKES.

As the saying goes, if you really think about it, there are no mistakes, only learnings. But if you don't have the strength to face up to what went wrong, you will either hide from others or make excuses for why things didn't go the way you'd planned. Worst of all, you may lie or try to shift blame.

None of these patterns are conducive to success in the long run, for you are sure to make the same mistakes once again. mental toughness helps you learn from your mistakes. We can learn a lot from our errors if we're ready to admit them and take the lessons that come with them to heart. Our knowledge of what is successful and what isn't comes from the errors we encounter daily. We miss out on innumerable chances to learn and grow if we don't make errors.

Ultimately, mental toughness teaches us that failures are stepping stones to perseverance. Adversity is a necessary ingredient for overcoming obstacles in life. We can't go ahead if we're stuck in the same location; therefore we need to be adaptable. We wouldn't be able to adapt when things don't go according to plan if we didn't make any errors. To succeed, we must be able to accept defeat.

MENTAL TOUGHNESS IS NECESSARY FOR YOU TO FACE YOUR FEARS WITH COURAGE.

It takes a lot to become aware of our shortcomings and to work outside our zone of comfort. As a matter of fact, you could say that mental toughness and courage are two sides of the same coin. You cannot have one without the other. Often, what we aspire towards involves accepting that we must work outside what we "conventionally like".

I can dream about being a CEO, but if I don't work on my people skills and continue to languish in front of the television in socks with a tub of popcorn, I know I'm not helping myself or feeding my aspirations.

Mental toughness gives you the courage to face your fears and to make decisions that may not always be in tune with your comfort zone of emotions. If you are someone who gets anxious in social settings, for example, mental toughness will give you the courage to step outside and tolerate these uncomfortable emotions.

As time passes, it becomes easier for you to become adept at social engagement. Discomfort plants the seeds for greater gains, and since mental toughness helps you tolerate that discomfort, it lays the groundwork for making a reality out of your aspirations.

Mental toughness helps you bounce back from your failures.

Again, each failure comes with a unique opportunity to learn what works and what doesn't. If you don't focus on building mental toughness, it can become a ground for you to give up before you reach your goals.

People who are psychologically tough bounce back from adverse situations more quickly than those who crumble. Failures are tools to build resilience, and you need mental toughness on both counts. The purpose of life is to help us develop and progress.

Throughout our lives, we are all connected by a thread of progress. We couldn't enhance our lives on every level if we didn't develop. Those who are mentally strong can take repeated failures without fear of humiliation because they have a solid sense of self-worth.

Strengthening your state of mind will allow you to see failure as an opportunity to learn and grow rather than a setback. It's only through the failures that we develop as people. We learn more about ourselves and the reasons behind the actions we take in our daily lives. As a result, we can put stressful events into perspective and get a deeper understanding of the world around us.

Finally, mental toughness helps you regulate your emotions.

Emotional lows and highs will be part of your pursuit of success. To be able to get to the end goal, you must strive for emotional balance. Without the skills of emotional regulation, you will give in to temptations and fail to take the necessary risks.

Mental toughness is necessary to control your emotions so that you don't give in to instant gratification or the impulses that often come when our emotions are on high alert. For example, after a week of eating healthy, you may take a break and eat out for a day. The next day, you know you have to return to your program, but your impulses keep pushing you to take another break and to eat out. Your emotions tell you that you can start eating healthy "tomorrow."

Your path to achievement will always be fraught with stumbling blocks and difficulties. Strengthening your mental fortitude can help you deal with life's inevitable disappointments with confidence.

Without mental toughness, like millions of others, you push your goals to "tomorrow," and the days pass, and you know how the rest unfolds. To be a leader, you have to keep your feet grounded in reality to achieve what your mind aspires to. This means that when necessary, logic must take precedence over emotion. mental toughness will help you get there.

COMPONENTS OF MENTAL TOUGHNESS

We've discussed why mental toughness is necessary to be successful in life. Once you develop grit, you set yourself up for making habits that stick and help you on the route to achieving your most excellent ends. With this being said, mental toughness has three important components—commitment/consistency, focus, and, you guessed it, self-confidence. Let's take a minute to look at what each means in relation to mental toughness.

Consistency

Motivation may help you get started on the road to success. You wake up on a beautiful morning and decide that now is the time to put your life back in proper working order. You are going to do amazing things. Your drive is great, and you are confident in your ability to complete the task. You put up your best efforts at work and in your personal life with the hope of achieving success in both areas. After a week, you begin to notice benefits, but not at the rate that you had anticipated. Your levels of motivation have plummeted to an all-time low.

This is the point at which you may either continue along the path to success or revert to your regular routine. To achieve your goals, you must maintain a continuous level of devotion. Consistency will aid you in overcoming burnouts, tiredness, doubts, and the impending dread of failure that will inevitably arise. Even on the days when your motivation is at its lowest ebb, dedication will keep your long-term aim in sight, and consistency will aid you in reaching your objective.

When you are mentally strong, you know what you want out of life and are dedicated to making that goal a reality on a constant basis. It doesn't bother you that you're deferring immediate fulfillment in favor of making selections that will ultimately satisfy your final aim. You are well aware that any setbacks you have are just transitory and have little chance of succeeding against your relentless efforts.

Focus

Our attention spans seem to be getting shorter by the second with contemporary living. There's a plethora of apps and shows and a thousand other distractions. Each distraction comes with a mini-distraction of its own! I noticed a curious cycle with my own patterns back when I was consistently studying myself. I'd set a goal to write four thousand words each day. I'd get distracted by a pop-up notification from YouTube and decide "a tiny break wouldn't hurt anyone." Then, one video would lead to another, and I'd be munching on countless snacks as I went down the tunnel of procrastination. Not only was I losing focus from work by watching YouTube, but I also wasn't even doing the watching mindfully because I was diverting attention between junk food and mindless entertainment.

A goldfish has an average attention span of nine seconds. A study done by Microsoft Corp. in 2015 found that people tend to lose concentration at the eight-second mark. The research noted that since their last survey in 2000 (back when the time mobiles and the internet were just taking over), human attention span had dropped from 12 seconds to just eight (McSpadden, 2015). This means that after eight seconds, you can legitimately get distracted by a hundred other environmental disturbances, more so if you lead a highly digitalized lifestyle.

This is just why you need mental toughness. Focusing on the work at hand is made possible by remaining in the current moment, focusing on the things you can control, and avoiding distractions that are unrelated to your performance. With a strong mind and a clear aim, you can resist the temptation to give in whenever anything comes along that distracts you. Getting more done is easier when you focus and concentrate on the activities that have the greatest impact.

Self-Confidence

Building self-confidence takes immense time and resilience. It necessitates that you develop the same love and compassion for yourself that you have for those close to you. A friend once asked me that when someone I love makes a mistake, do I berate them in such a way that they completely lose all self-confidence? When I responded with "never," they asked, *"if you wouldn't berate them for a mistake, why would you constantly demean yourself when you make one? Isn't it a known fact that mistakes will happen? Shouldn't they make you believe you have the strength to face whatever comes even more?"*

That was food for thought—and I realized that each thought we nourish has a message that we send to our minds and bodies about our capability to meet a challenge. Mental toughness helps you build unshakeable belief in your capacity to accomplish a goal. I realize that one mistake or setback was never definitive of my goal—and neither was a hundred, so long as I was still trying to get where I'd set out to go.

My bad days stopped defining me, and I could use the failures as lessons and the mistakes as feedback on what

I could do differently next time. When you build mental toughness, you hone a fierce fire of confidence that makes you want to achieve your goal with more intensity, passion, and commitment.

Truthfully, mental toughness isn't one quality but a balance between all we discussed. Along with this, you need to remember that it isn't something you build in a day. You cannot go from being a social recluse to someone who spends time hanging out with friends with absolute ease the very next day. The balance you need takes time to develop, and you will get there with enough practice.

Building mental toughness is a strength skill in itself and one that you must devote your energies to achieve. You're all you have got. Best make the ride worthwhile. Here are some tips to help you along the way.

- Practice, practice, practice. If you have a big workshop coming up, practice for it weeks ahead. If you have a meeting, an exam, a rehearsal, a show, an exhibition, or even if you just need to stay home and cook a meal for your family, the more time you spend learning your craft, the better you will become at it.
- Orient your negative thoughts so that they take positive forms. Rather than thinking, *"this is too*

hard, I cannot do it," tell yourself, *"I will take this as a challenge, and it will help me get better and better."* It will still be difficult, but the more you convince yourself that you have what it takes, the more you'll find that you *really do have what it takes.*

- Whenever you feel the negative thoughts overwhelm you, take a few deep breaths. Remind yourself that the day you decided you were going to do this is the day *you became ready to do it as well.* You are worth the goal and the greatness that it will bring to your life. Run your hand over a solid surface, count to ten as slowly as you can, and think, *"I am here. I am ready."*

- Keep a written note of all your goals. When you do this, write little encouraging notes that you will be able to fall back on when you are not as motivated to keep going. Look at these goals and notes of encouragement every day before you sleep.

- Be in the company of positive people who will not criticize and scrutinize every move that you make. There's nothing like the downward tug of a negative person, and you can do without the feeling of hopelessness that it brings. When they say, *"your vibe decides your tribe,"* they mean it—so keep yourself positive and attract those who will keep you in the light.

- Narrow down on a small mantra. To this day, whenever I am too stressed, I close my eyes and chant "Om" ten times with deep breaths. Your mantra can be an encouraging line, a religious phrase, or any other word that has spiritual connotations or grounds you to the reality of your existence. Use this mantra as a fortification to keep yourself calm and happy.

- Stay light, and don't make something too serious out of this life. Smile often, and whenever you can. Release the negative energy that can become a pit of poison in your body, and be your most authentic self.

- Finally, believe in yourself. This one is going to take the most work because it's often easier to live in doubt than it is to do the work needed to build self-belief. But keep going, and the more you cultivate self-belief, the more doable everything else will become.

We human beings tend to have a little quirk. I'm not generalizing anything here, but I speak from experience when I say that many among us take things at face value. So, when we see a shiny photo of a social media influencer with a body that looks like it's been carved from moonlight and read a caption like, "born with mental toughness," we immediately look at the quality and the individual as one and unreachable. "mental toughness" becomes definitive of a heavily photoshopped and filtered picture that seems perfect and therefore not something we are entitled to, since we apparently aren't born with it.

Well, this is just not right.

But wait, for there are more myths surrounding the concept of mental toughness. Before I tell you why they don't count, let's take a little look at a few of them.

MYTHS ABOUT MENTAL TOUGHNESS

The most accepted definition of "myth" is a widely accepted but completely false idea. So if you have spent time believing any of the myths that we'll talk about here, don't beat yourself up. We've all been there. What matters is that you dispel them now, and move forward with the best of your intentions.

Myth One: You either have mental toughness, or you don't.

It doesn't work that way. The very traits of mental toughness are consistency and commitment, and these are not talents you are born with, but rather tools that you develop to better your trade.

Rather than looking at everything from an "if" perspective (*if I have a good body, I can become a model*) look at things from a "how much" perspective (*how much time do I devote to developing a healthy body?*) to set long-term goals for yourself.

When it comes to the core components of mental toughness, they need to be *learned.* You can begin today or tomorrow, but the fact is that the sooner you begin, the more adept you'll get. If you use the "I either have it or don't" approach, you'll keep pushing this learning to a later stage, which will make the goal fall further out of reach. Believe in yourself and get to work. I promise you can get there.

Myth Two: If it ain't broke, why waste time fixing it?

The bane of human existence is living inside the comfort zone without ever attempting to step out. As time passes, we become so set in our ways that the mere thought of doing something out of turn becomes frightful. I know of people who were not able to fulfill their lifelong dreams of getting on a plane to Paris, of going to that cooking school they always dreamt of, and of never taking a chance on themselves because

"I'm too comfortable at home. Who knows what I'll face outside?"

Erin Hanson is known for many things, one among them being the famous quote, *"What if I fall? But oh, my darling, what if you fly?"* The fact is—if you don't step outside the norm of what you're used to, you'll never know what could be different. The "ifs" and "buts" will always remain just so, and you will continue to remain wishful of things that never came to be.

Mental toughness is necessary for you because it teaches you to look at and aspire to life outside this comfort zone. Never goad yourself into thinking it isn't necessary, for, without it, life loses purpose.

Myth Three: Mental toughness is just about training your mind

Training your mind is undoubtedly important, but our minds and bodies are intrinsically connected. If you focus on only one aspect, the system crashes. Your priority should be on honing skills that influence all aspects of your performance.

This includes encouraging positive self-talk, spending time in nature, eating healthy, taking walks, doing mindfulness exercises, sleeping right, and enjoying time with friends and family.

Of course you will train your mind to do all these things, but you should also know when to listen to your body. There are days when physical exhaustion can be very real and very pervasive, and being tuned to your body's needs will help you give it the care and love it deserves.

For instance, if you have the tendency to engage in negative self-talk, you have to train your mind to focus on encouraging yourself. But if, at the start of something momentous, your body responds with a physical reaction like arrhythmia, you *also need to train your body to cope with situations of stress.*

Myth Four: Mental toughness is built alone

Only, it isn't. Without constructive feedback and support paving your way, it'll be doubly hard to build mental toughness. With this being said, not all of us come from the same circumstances. I've known people who've been forced into corners by society, but worked on their mental toughness and risen to positions of power nonetheless.

The key here is not the idea of "needing appreciation and encouragement" from others, but acting in ways that elicit their feedback, whether harsh or constructive. When you have this feedback, it's possible for you to evaluate your goals and path from a long-term perspective.

You learn to differentiate between people who're just being petty, and those who are truly looking out for you. So, mental toughness isn't built alone. It rests a lot upon how you process feedback and translate it into your future decisions and actions. The more you hone your skills from a constructive perspective, the more your chances for success.

Myth Five: Mental toughness means ignoring emotions

On the contrary, ignoring emotions is a sign of a mentally fragile person. When you ignore something, you're either too afraid to face it, or you think you don't have the resources to cope with it. Mental toughness isn't about ignoring your emotions, it's about *acknowledging and facing them, irrespective of how tough this may be at times.*

The true mark of a mentally tough human being is that they have faced the fire as diamonds in the rough, and come out with incredible sheen. This requires finding constructive and helpful ways to handle tough emotions that can be distracting. Mentally tough people also know how to harness emotions like anger and frustration to useful ends—you use your inner fire to propel you towards higher success.

Myth Six: Stress doesn't affect mentally tough people

Everybody feels stress and frustration. These are universal emotions, but mentally tough people know how to channel these emotions and compartmentalize their work-life schedules. They don't get overwhelmed by the weight of stress and throw in the towel. They keep their priorities intact, and while stress is perennial, they know that the way to balance is out is via healthy eating, optimum rest, and an overall state of wellbeing. These are qualities that they actively invest in.

Myth Seven: Failure doesn't exist in mentally tough peoples' dictionaries

Just like stress, failure is universal. As is the dread that comes with it. The difference between mentally tough people and others is that they take the failures in their stride, and use the lessons learned from them to fuel their eventual actions and decisions. They treat failure as the opportunity to understand "what can be done differently next time," for life is equal parts success and learning. It's not that the word "failure" is missing from their dictionary, only, they have changed the meaning from *"lack of success"* to *"opportunity to learn."*

Ultimately, everything you do boils down to making a choice. If you choose to commit to becoming a mentally strong person, you are already 50% there. I always like to say that when the mind is convinced, the body will follow. At each point, you need to make a choice about what you need, and what you want. The power to make decisions is in your hands, and you have the lasting capacity to make something out of what you decide. What will guide you along the way is self-discipline.

SO, WHAT IS SELF-DISCIPLINE?

Here's a little secret most people won't tell you. The biggest wars, the ones that have the capacity to ravage us and leave us cold, are often the ones that *we wage with ourselves.* For most of us, self-discipline does not happen in a linear direction. It's ensconced in good intentions, but we often procrastinate. We push important goals to a "tomorrow" that never comes, and each day the temptation of instant gratification overpowers our senses and takes us down a rabbit hole of "two-minute" pleasure and lasting guilt. I empathize.

Some of life's hardest choices include getting up to write a paper or putting in another hour of work to meet a deadline when you're faced with the alternative of a comfortable bed and soft pillows calling out your name. When faced with the prospect of either going to the gym or ordering pizza, the natural instinct for many of us would be *pizza today, gym tomorrow.*

Instant gratification is a dangerous game. We live in an age of convenience. Having desires met with lightning speeds isn't necessarily evil. However, within the context of this age and how wired we have become to quick-fix solutions, instant gratification can lead to harmful impulsive behaviors that take away from our quality of living and overall health.

Science itself states that the human brain is constantly changing in reaction to the things we do and prioritize. So, every time you seek to fulfill a craving for junk food by ordering in instantly, the neural pathways in your brain for this act of gratification get reinforced and become stronger. The result is that whenever you picture junk food in your brain again, you immediately feel the urge to call your local takeout joint and order from there. This makes it next to impossible to break the cycle. What you essentially develop is a terrible habit.

In place, what you should be working towards is self-discipline. I know it sounds less appealing than the prospect of a cheesy pizza or two scoops of your favorite ice cream delivered to you whenever you want it, but it's not just me saying this. Research shows that people with self-discipline are happier in the long run.

Do a little exercise truthfully. The next time you give in to a craving and order something when you shouldn't be, think, *really think,* how long does the pleasure from getting it last? From my personal experience, I've seen that whenever I ordered food that I wasn't supposed to or spent lump sum amounts buying things I don't need, all I felt was two minutes of pleasure before being wracked with guilt and remorse, which itself propelled further destructive spending. How is that a way to be happy?

On the other hand, people who exhibit more self-control don't waste as much time on whether it's okay to invest in habits or routines that will take away from their optimum state of existence for "a few minutes" or "just a day." They are not governed by their impulses. Rather, they choose to move ahead of these impulses and question the necessity of something before investing in it. This results in level-headed choices which lead to long-term satisfaction. The watchword doesn't remain, *"I ate a pizza and felt good for a bit but I wasted a full day of exercising and dieting,"* rather, it becomes *"I chose my health over junk food today, and I feel proud about that."*

Obviously, the pride that comes from the latter choice outshines the few minutes of pleasure you get while wolfing down on something because you gave in to your impulses.

With this being said, developing self-discipline is an exercise in itself. Here are some things you can do to get started.

Acknowledge your weaknesses

Whether it's junk food or snacks or procrastinating on deadlines, whatever your shortcomings may be, own them. Too often, the biggest mistake we make is shunning the notion that we have problems. This makes us push all issues under the rug. Ironically, we take guilty pleasure in repeating the same behaviors that get us down.

When faced with their consequences, we become surprised because we never acknowledged their existence in the first place. This leads to shifting blame upon the world. *"Why is the world so cruel to me," "I didn't deserve that," "It's not my fault if I'm not losing weight."* This shifting blame becomes problematic because it makes us blind to the root cause of our setbacks. The first step in overcoming any flaw is acknowledging its existence.

Remove temptations from near sight

There's an old adage that says once something is out of sight, it is also out of mind. This may not always apply, but it's true that the impact or craving to indulge in something unhealthy is reduced when it's not within your immediate line of vision. It's a simple sentence, yet it's full of wisdom. Self-control may be substantially improved by simply eliminating the things that entice you the most from your surroundings.

Don't purchase fast food if you really want to attain better health. Keep your phone in silent mode while at work to boost your productivity. If you get distracted by online shopping apps, keep a minimum of them on your phone screen. Go shopping in stores instead of browsing things online. It's easier to fulfill your objectives when there are less distractions around you. Get rid of negative influences in your life so that you can achieve your goals.

Plan and execute your goals systematically

Having a clear picture of what you want to achieve can help you acquire self-discipline with greater efficiency. If you decide at random that "I just want a healthy body," you'll be lost for what to do. Instead, be systematic.

Lay down the foundation of what you want as "good health" and subdivide your short and long-term goals under this. Short-term goals can include losing ten pounds in the next three months, and long-term goals can include things like coming out of a prediabetic state. In order to achieve your objectives, you must have a detailed strategy.

You might easily get lost or become diverted if you are unsure of your objective. You need to figure out your identity and what you stand for. Make a motto for yourself to help you stay on track. Use this method to keep yourself on track and set a clear goal. Having a clear idea of your definition of success is also essential.

Work towards building self-discipline

Self-discipline is not a trait we are born with. Rather, it's something we build. If you want to become better at any talent, you'll need to perfect it every day. Willpower and self-discipline are much like going to the gym: they require a lot of effort, but once you set your mind to it, results are inevitable.

Self-discipline involves a lot of work and attention, which may be exhausting. In the digital age, it's so easy to fall off track and think that a day lost won't matter, we can always try again the next day. Unfortunately, one day often builds to many, because once we fall off the wagon, the ride departs. It becomes doubly difficult to begin again.

No matter what, you need to keep the big picture in mind. If you procrastinate, all you do is move further away from your goal. Be diligent in your pursuits, and you will get there.

Make practical and simple habits

In the beginning, learning self-discipline and cultivating a new habit might seem overwhelming, particularly if you focus on the whole undertaking. If you don't want to feel overwhelmed, keep things simple. Consider breaking down your aim into manageable chunks. Do one thing every day and develop self-discipline with that objective in mind instead of seeking to change too much too soon.

Begin exercising twenty minutes a day if you want to become fitter. If you're just starting out, a twenty-minute walk will suffice. If you're trying to sleep early, begin by going to bed ten minutes earlier than you usually do. This also means switching off all distractions (including your phone) ten minutes ahead of bedtime.

For those who are trying to eat better, start by preparing your lunch for the next day the night before. Begin with little steps and work your way up. When you're ready, you can increase the minutes, a little at a time. This is no sprint, it's a marathon. You're preparing for the bigger goals, so remember that the time you invest is worth it.

Rewire your belief systems

I can sum up this point in one line—*"believe, and you can."*

A Stanford University research study found that a person's beliefs influence how much willpower they have (Steakley, 2011). In order to break beyond your own self-imposed limitations, it is necessary to think that you have the capacity for self-discipline. Putting a cap on your self-control will only cause you to burn out before you reach your objectives. Basically, the more you think that you have what it takes, the more realistic the objective will become.

In other words, it's possible that how much willpower and self-control we have is based on our own internal views of these abilities. If you can eliminate your internal hurdles and sincerely think that you can achieve something, then you will be motivated to push ahead, no matter what the circumstances are.

Plan A is great, but make a Plan B anyway

Within psychology, there exists a great little term called "implementation intention." The beauty of this term is that it always allows you to have a backup. You have a goal intention which denotes a desired future state via *"I intend to achieve this goal."* So, if your goal is to lose weight, you keep more than one option open each day.

The mere act of goal setting or wanting to achieve it badly isn't enough to attain it, right? To get there, you actually need to *act*. Let's say you planned to exercise today by going for a run outdoors. You wake up and find it's raining cats and dogs. Without a Plan B, your goal-setting for the day is ruined! Instead, "implementation intention" allows you to keep a backup through "if" and "then" statements. In this case, you make two plans.

- Plan A: If it is sunny, I will go running.
- Plan B: If it rains, I will exercise by watching a HIIT video on YouTube.

It's truly as simple as that. The result is that you get to achieve your goal for the day, even if the means are different. If your goal was to work out for thirty minutes, keeping two plans in place doubles your chances of fulfilling it.

One of the most important qualities you need if you want to build mental toughness is self-discipline. The latter ensures that you keep going in pursuit of your higher goals, no matter what the circumstances. So, if you want to lose ten pounds but are getting tempted at the sight of a hot fudge sundae, self-discipline will help you make the difficult choice of keeping the sundae aside for your bigger goal—a healthy life.

BENEFITS OF CULTIVATING SELF-DISCIPLINE AS A HABIT

As Warren Buffett once said, *"We don't have to be smarter than the rest, we have to be more disciplined than them."* Let's take a look at how self-discipline can help us.

Self-discipline gives us the grit we need to do what we *must be doing.* Sometimes, putting off things that give us instant gratification can be hard. But if we give in to temptations all the time, we only thwart our progress. Self-discipline keeps us grounded and helps us look forward, always in pursuit of the goals we initially set for ourselves. I spoke about Angela Duckworth's research. I'll refer to it again, in particular, her statement that to achieve difficult goals, you need more than talent. What really helps is the *sustained and focused application of your talents over time* (Duckworth, 2016), or in other words, cultivating self-discipline.

We often procrastinate when we get stressed. Negative emotions can tempt us to put off working towards our goals and lean on instant comfort—be it an unhealthy snack, not studying for the rest of the day, or giving in to watching a series when we should be working. However, research has found that self-discipline is helpful in keeping students focused on their goals and overcoming anxiety. In other words, when you have self-discipline, you don't allow anxiety to get the better of you because you know that no matter what, the goal is worth fighting for.

You should develop self-discipline as a habit if you want better health. It enables you to stay away from harmful distracting devices like alcohol and cigarettes. You also don't feel the urge to binge on fast food whenever you feel anxious or need a distraction. Self-discipline ensures that you work methodically for something without giving in to the stress that can make us turn to junk food. Your health remains intact. Additionally, if you cultivate self-discipline and you decide to spend an hour each day doing physical activities, the former will help you stick to the latter goal, therefore leading to optimum overall physical and mental health.

Self-discipline takes you above arrogance to understand other people's perspectives. You value their input and take their emotions into account. This impacts positively on relationships.

Resilience is often an off-shoot of developing self-discipline. Resilience helps you build faith in your skills and rely on your strengths to navigate through life's challenging circumstances. You understand that even if you encounter issues, you will bounce back because life is big, and every misstep is an opportunity to learn something new.

Last but just as important, self-discipline makes you happy. You don't begrudge others for what they have because you are too busy *building a successful future for yourself.* Making you productive keeps your creative spirit alive and makes you look at how you can constantly better yourself. It does not have any room for petty jealousies or anger or frustration about "why do I have so little?" By helping you control and channel your behavior in appropriate directions, self-discipline influences your well-being and makes you upbeat.

CULTIVATING SELF-DISCIPLINE IS POSSIBLE

It is possible for all of us to cultivate self-discipline. It is a habit, after all! And all habits can be built. They begin as routines, and once we rely on a routine every day, it is bound to turn into a habit. The trick is to look at self-discipline in the same light as you'd see an essential daily function like drinking water or eating food. When it becomes part of your "necessary things to do every day," it will come through for you no matter what. Here are some ways in which you can initiate the process.

- Cultivate passion in what you do. If you do things with love, you will be disciplined. We get distracted and annoyed when we have to do things we don't like. If your end goal is something you want with all your heart, you'll have the discipline to push through all the tasks needed to get to this goal.
- Begin by making a daily schedule of your activities. Then, take a moment to think about what you appreciate and if your actions are consistent with those principles. Many activities you engage in on a daily basis undoubtedly violate these ideals. Set goals and work steadily toward achieving them once you've identified potential issues.
- Self-discipline boils down to a personal decision. In every instant, you must determine whether to carry out your responsibilities or just carry out your desires. Successful people are those who can examine the facts at hand

and then make decisions based on what they've
learned.

- Make a list of specific objectives that you can
  accomplish. It's a lot easier to achieve your
  goals if you can see yourself reaching them. In
  order to reach a goal, it is important to write it
  down.

- Keep your distractions aside when you are
  doing something. Eat mindfully, sleep
  peacefully, and work methodically. Our
  generation is far too focused on constant
  distractions. We need to watch TV shows when
  we eat, browse the internet when we should be
  sleeping, and constantly check social media
  when we are supposed to be working.
  Eliminate these distractions and focus on doing
  the things you have set out to do with the full
  force of your concentration. Set timelines and
  goals like—*"I will work for an hour without
  checking social media." "I will turn off my phone
  thirty minutes before I go to sleep." "I will enjoy the
  food I eat and focus on its taste and sensations rather
  than watching TV."*

- Be proud of your progress. Getting distracted
  and rewarding progress isn't the same thing.
  You do the latter mindfully. Take breaks once in
  a while and go out in the open to take a walk.

Cook something good for yourself, learn a new skill and always tell yourself that you are doing wonderfully.

- Tackle the difficult things first. This will set your focus straight, and you can handle the other tasks with relative ease.
- Make decisions and be responsible for them. Don't try to change your natural rhythm. Work when you're most productive. Do what works best for your own schedule.
- Visualize! After you lose weight, imagine yourself wearing the outfit you've always wanted to wear. It is much simpler to push through fear and doubt when you have a clear picture of what you want to achieve in your mind's eye.

Self-discipline and mental toughness are two sides of the same coin, and one is essential for the other. When it comes to developing mental toughness, understanding how it works can help. Let's take a minute to study this.

HOW DOES MENTAL TOUGHNESS WORK?

Like anything else that must be honed, mental toughness begins as a routine that can transcend into a habit with enough practice. It is cultivated through visualization techniques and positive self-talk.

Routines

Routines are essential for mental toughness. They help us to keep the faith in the process without worrying about how the end result will turn out. In turn, being devoted to the process ensures that the end result is nothing but optimum. Routines also save us from falling into the trap of overthinking. Mental toughness results from not worrying about "things that are unseen or may or may not happen in the future." By helping us focus on the present without fretting over past mistakes or stressing about the future, routines help us cultivate discipline and mental toughness.

Visualizations

Mental toughness results from the inspiration garnered through visualization. By keeping a clear idea of what you want to achieve, you set your mind on doing all that is necessary to get there. For example, if your visualization is something abstract like, *"I want to look good,"* it can make it very difficult to form specific goals. What goals will help you look good? This causes a lapse in mental toughness because you're unsure of what to do. But if you have a measurable, observable vision like, *"I see myself with six-packs,"* it helps you attune your aspirations and practical skills to *achieve this specific vision.*

Even if the cards are heavily against you, visualization will develop your mental toughness, which will help you maintain your composure and optimism. It's critical to see the bright side of things while still being open to the possibility of the unanticipated happening. Visualizations should be thorough and define exactly what you intend to accomplish while keeping headspace for uncertainty and variations in plans. If you want the vision badly enough, mental toughness is bound to guide your way.

Affirmations/positive self-talk

Positive affirmations can be a great aid in developing mental toughness. Negative ideas may be overcome with the use of affirmations, which are precise, positive phrases. Through the power of visualizations and self-belief, good changes in your work and personal life may be made. Affirmations assist you to overcome mental hurdles since they are based on the premise that how you perceive the world and yourself influences what you do and how you behave.

Tailor your affirmations to come across as positive statements that help you get over a lack of self-confidence. You'd use phrases like "I'm capable of achieving prosperity or success is attracted to me" in this context.

Your subconscious mind will register this statement whenever you repeat it with conviction and increase your self-confidence. What you achieve from here is genuine faith in your abilities and the desire to strengthen them using mental toughness. What you believe influences your actions. The more happy and upbeat you feel as a result of repeating this affirmation, the more mental toughness you'll have.

At this stage, you may be wondering—*"Do I really need this? What if I already have all the mental toughness I require?"* Well, there are certain signs that point to the adequacy or otherwise of your mental toughness levels. Before we conclude this chapter, let's look at what some of these signs are.

SIGNS YOU MAY LACK MENTAL TOUGHNESS AND HOW TO STOP THEM

We may wake up and decide that the world is our oyster—but mental toughness dictates that you must know *how to order your own life first.* You should be able to lead yourself before you even think of commanding others. This means establishing control over the way you talk, how you carry yourself, the things you put into your body, the choices you make, and the changes you visualize. This requires enormous discipline, which can be difficult to cultivate. But think about what happens when you do. *Every difficult aspiration becomes achievable when you get to this level of discipline. It is the only way to develop mental toughness.*

People lacking mental toughness often look at failure as the end of everything. The belief that you can't fail isn't going to stop you from failing, but it may keep you from ever trying to do things. Mentally tough people understand that failure is as inevitable as success, and sometimes you need a hundred failures to achieve one momentous success. They see failure as a springboard on the path to achievement. Setbacks don't bother them since they know they can bounce back from them.

An important determinant of lacking mental toughness is feeling guilty for your accomplishments or dreaming big. If others are putting you down or saying "you've got your head in the clouds," know that they have nothing on you. Do not apologize for the commitment and discipline you have towards your goals.

If others make you feel that you don't deserve the successes you gain because of your hard work, shun their negative influences. Mental toughness also means that we cut off those relationships which do nothing but bring us down. There's joy in uplifting others, so do that often. But never tear yourself down based on someone else's judgment of you.

Don't hide behind your insecurities. A sign you lack mental strength is that you put up a jaunty, overconfident exterior while you are full of insecurities within. Acknowledge your shortcomings because they are part of your intrinsic being, and work through them to become the best version of yourself. Own who you are, and don't spend your energy covering your weaknesses. Rather, use your time and skills to improve yourself constantly.

Finally, mentally fragile people often suppress their emotions. They think that expressing fear or happiness or sorrow are signs of weakness. But mentally tough people know that owning their fear is fine, and they also don't feel destabilized because something has hurt them. They monitor and evaluate their emotions instead of shunning them. They're conscious of how their sentiments impact their thinking and actions, leveraging this to their advantage. When you do this, it allows you to understand what situation precipitated into making you feel bad. You can then work through this so that this situation is not repeated again.

Moving ahead, we will discuss some skills you need to build that will help you in becoming mentally tough. In the next chapter, we'll talk about the first skill—

unbreakability. Before that, I'll sum up the key points we covered in this chapter.

CHAPTER SUMMARY

- Mental toughness is a life skill that will help you achieve lasting progress and overall well-being.
- Mental toughness is the result of consistency, focus, and self-confidence.
- Being mentally tough means accepting that failure is essential to achieving success.
- Routines, visualizations, and positive self-affirmations can help you develop mental toughness.
- Irrespective of your physical and cognitive talents, mental toughness is what will help you in the ultimate pursuit of your goals.

2

MENTAL TOUGHNESS SKILL I: UNBREAKABILITY

"You may not control all the events that happen to you, but you can decide not to be reduced by them."

— MAYA ANGELOU

Let me begin this chapter by sharing an incident from a couple of years back. I had already made up my mind to tread a path of wellbeing and strength. Against all odds, I was doing okay. My job was going well, I had finally found that elusive work-life balance, and I had time to enjoy life with my family. I began thinking that my years of hard work were finally paying off. The COVID-19 pandemic struck in 2019, but I didn't overthink it.

I was staying home, putting in the hours, and keeping myself grounded. One day, I got a call from my best friend's wife. She told me that Drew had been unwell for a while, and he had caught the virus. This was the boy I'd grown up with, shared classes and pubescent problems with, and the boy I'd imagined sticking by my side as we grew old together. I felt the ground beneath my feet shift, change focus, and become liquid.

The day he was sent to the ICU was the toughest one by far. It was a tough time. The pandemic made it impossible for me to see him—all our interactions were virtual. I felt very near crumbling. I called his mom and asked her how she was coping. She told me, *"I'm staying strong because if I don't, he won't."* That's when the power of unbreakability hit me. I heard the strength in her voice—unwavering and comforting. I chose to imbibe that strength within myself. I prayed for Drew, and I stayed strong for him.

Drew recovered. And I learned something valuable in the process of watching him fight and beat the virus. Unbreakability is one of the most crucial life skills you can acquire. Tough times will never stop coming, for life moves in a constant ebb and flow between the good and the bad. But when you build yourself to weather any storm, you know that no matter how tough the going gets, you will keep moving towards the better end, the higher goal, the ultimate pursuit.

UNBREAKABILITY IS A VIRTUE

What do you immediately think of when I say the word "unbreakability"? If you ask me, my instant response is—*"resilience—knowing that difficulties will always exist and I won't be successful all the time, but also knowing that I will work my way around all situations because life is too beautiful to be wasted living in fear and inadequacy."* That is my definition of unbreakability. Let's take a look at what the theory on the topic says as well.

In his work *"Resilience theory: Theoretical and professional conceptualizations. Journal of Human Behavior in the Social Environment,"* Greene writes that unbreakability/resilience refers to all the circumstances that lead to successful consequences when someone is faced with adversity. His approach to understanding unbreakability looks at prospective risks for subsequent behavioral issues and the protective principles that can shield or reduce individuals from damaging environmental influences. His categorical definition of unbreakability within this perspective is—unbreakability/resilience represents the prowess to overcome adversities and attain success even with exposure to high-risk factors (Greene, 2003).

On the same lines, another definition of unbreakability is that it is resourceful acclimatization to changes in the circumstances of one's existence. This change in circumstances includes environmental eventualities (Block & Block, 1980). It can also be taken to mean the ability to recover and maintain adaptive behavior in the wake of initial fear or incapacity happening due to a stressful situation (Gamezy, 1991).

To simplify things, you can look at the concept of unbreakability as descriptive of the differences in individual responses to situations of stress and adversity. Unbreakable people know that the problems will pass. On the other hand, each problem will weaken fragile people until they break down.

Did you notice the commonalities in all the definitions and explanations I shared above? There's the universal acknowledgment of three things—

- Stressful situations will happen.
- Environmental and internal changes are inevitable.
- People who adapt to these changes and stresses are the ones who remain unbroken by life's trials and open to enjoying the good things.

Does this mean that unbreakable people don't feel loss or pain or frustration? Of course, they do! But they know how to compartmentalize these feelings and ensure that they do not get in the way of routine existence. They go about living as they always have without lending extra importance to the stressful situation— and with time, the situation passes, and their life flows in a solid, consistent fashion.

The difference is not in terms of how unfortunate circumstances make us "feel"- all of us feel burdened at times—but in choosing how to *react to these circumstances.* As the saying goes, you can either run the day or let the day run you. If you choose the latter, however, you will not only give in to all stresses but also go to bed anxious, tired, and frustrated. Seriously, who wants that?

Unbreakability comes through as a personal, individualistic trait that allows you to adapt and cope. It promotes your survival and at times, even lets you thrive in challenging situations. Eric D. Miller, the author of *"Reconceptualizing the Role of Resiliency in Coping and Therapy,"* also states that if you are highly adaptable and focused on listening to the voice of your inner logic, you can even wield the trauma of stressful situations and use it to grow and flourish (Miller, 2003).

Flourishing in all situations is perhaps one of the most beautiful things about unbreakable people. If they practice and lean on their resilience consistently, they learn to channel and use trauma like a sword. They gain knowledge of their inner selves from this trauma and become truly indomitable beings. There is immense strength in that.

In a paper that came out in 2004, Peterson and Seligman built a classification system for understanding what we categorize as being a "strength" and a "virtue." This system comprises eight main criteria. To be a virtue/strength, a human quality must:

1. Lead to fulfilling events that would categorize an overall "good life" both for you and for those who are close to you;
2. Contribute value that goes beyond just adding to your financial wealth;
3. Keep you humble (so you don't diminish others in your presence or when displaying your skills);
4. Be steady in the face of temptation to easy alteration (for instance, if happiness is a virtue, it cannot give way to despair within seconds);
5. Be measurable concerning behavior and open to display as a human characteristic;
6. Have distinct differences from other virtues;

7. Be a measure of distinction for people who possess it (that is, people with the virtue are looked up to because they display and have it);

8. Come across as a treasured trait to be cultivated and sustained within a larger societal institution (such as a family cultivating the virtue of humility or compassion.)

Based on these criteria, six main categories were designated as the parental terms for all virtues—wisdom, and knowledge; humanity; justice; courage; temperance, and transcendence (Peterson & Seligman, 2004). Within each category, you have different virtues. For instance, the "courage" category encapsulates virtues like bravery, perseverance, persistence, authenticity, energy, and industriousness. It is important to understand unbreakability from this perspective because it gives you the knowledge of whether it can qualify as one of the highest human traits.

If you think about it, unbreakability/ resilience meets more or less all the criteria we talked about. It leads to the overall sound quality of life, contributes to your mental and physical wellbeing, and helps you stay strong in the face of adversity without letting you give in to fear and nervousness—which are often the more accessible options. It is something we admire in others. And it is an observable and valuable human characteristic. When you see or interact with someone who is unbreakable, you draw inspiration and the urge to display similar traits—to be as indomitable in the face of adversity.

Have you ever heard the word *"eudaimonia?"* I discovered the word in the course of reading literature for this book, and I must say, there's a special connection between unbreakability and engendering eudaimonia. It is synonymous with *human flourishing,* or a state of existence where you are at peace with yourself, content, and happy. By shielding you and offering you the means to overcome trauma and stresses in your life, unbreakability has the power to become a super-virtue of sorts. It helps internalize the notion that *you deserve peace and happiness, and you are going to acquire them yourself, no matter how tough the times may get.*

From this perspective, while resilience has traits related to both survival and endurance, it is a few steps ahead of both of them. It is endurance that has found a direction. It is taking the total of your hardships, even the ones which will leave permanent scars, and using them to enrich and build on your life experiences. It is saying and acting on, *"Life gets tough, but that doesn't make it any less worth living."*

Which brings me to the next question. Do resilient people remain the same, no matter the extent of their hardships? If you ask me, no. If we keep equating unbreakability with "bouncing back from trauma and living the same life we used to," we fail to account for the impact of a challenging situation—and the impact often leads to immense growth. We may not always bounce back. We may not always go back to the old selves—the people we used to be before the hardship struck us. All the families who said goodbye to their loved ones via plexiglass windows during the pandemic are never getting them back. Lives change, and sometimes trauma is too significant and too pervasive to simply shun aside.

Sometimes, the best, the strongest, and the most resolute thing we can do is move ahead. Being unbreakable is not synonymous with going back to our past selves. It is in embracing and accepting things that have come to pass. It is using new experiences to better our understanding of ourselves and the world around us.

What's the point in so much? What's the point in enduring when you can just sit and wallow in self-pity? Well, you ask yourself. You have two options.

1. *I will love this life because I am alive, I am breathing, and I can make something beautiful of it.*
2. *I will spend my life being controlled by situations and feeling miserable all the time.*

One of these options takes hard work, but the results are so worth it. Which one would you choose?

THE IMPORTANCE OF UNBREAKABILITY IN WORK AND BUSINESS

Why do we need to show strength in our workspaces? Well, the natural answer is that our work environments are often stressful, and we need our mental faculties on our side if we are to cope with this stress regularly. If every strenuous event that happened in our jobs caused us anxiety or anguish, how would we reach success?

Success isn't something that comes to those who never stumble—it comes to those who are willing to get back up, brush off the dust of the last encounter, and work doubly smart to get where they need to go. A study conducted by a leading job board called CV-Library discovered that 57% of employees feel unbreakability/resilience is a core skill for employment. 71% acknowledged adaptability (which encapsulates unbreakability) as crucial (Gentle, 2019), revealing that businesses value employees who have grit and are not afraid of a challenge.

The reason why businesses prefer unbreakable employees is apparent—they are more motivated and have a greater ability to deal with changes. They also don't burn out as easily, therefore staying in good health. Being unbreakable also means that the mental health of employees remains intact even after difficult situations, making the workplace a zone where they can give their best each day. What results are a regular presence and solid output. With this being said, let's look at some reasons why unbreakability is such an asset in the workspace.

Unbreakability is key in **handling challenging workplace situations**. It prevents negative emotions and the notion of "everyone is out to get me" from interfering with logical judgment. Instead of harboring self-pity, it gives employees the ability to see things from a calm perspective and come up with solutions. Instead of looking for who to shift blame to, it makes them focus on finding a common route to lasting solutions.

The more adaptable and unbreakable a person is, **the more confident they are**. They are far more inclined to speak out and participate, and better able to express themselves accurately and productively. Collaboration among employees is essential in a company if it is to fully explore all possibilities and foster inventiveness— and unbreakability ensures that employees leave their personal agendas aside for the collective good of the company.

Businesses can't operate well without unbreakability. **Businesses that can adapt well to transitions and have employees who work well together will be the ones to survive the tough times.** Managers will always prefer to retain employees who have patience and are able to accept required adjustments. Workers that are more tolerant of change are also likely to stick around in spite of troubles.

When a person loses his or her enthusiasm for their job, he or she becomes exhausted. This is often associated with being fragile and looking for a way out all the time. Unbreakability is a skill that may help individuals **stay on to the passion they have for their work and give it their all.** If you are motivated to stick to the grind on a daily basis, success will find its way to you no matter how long the wait is.

Unbreakability will help you develop **realistic work expectations.** Too often, we keep our heads in the clouds and forget to ground ourselves to reality. We expect too much from ourselves and our colleagues, forgetting to communicate clearly and set proper boundaries. Unbreakability helps us identify that "this is the limit—this is the total of what I can do, and do well." We need knowledge of that boundary so that we don't get exploited by the whims of others as well. Unbreakability is crucial to standing up for ourselves in the workplace even if the going gets tough. This ensures that expectations don't go beyond capabilities, allowing for efficient progress.

A growth attitude encourages a willingness to receive and provide feedback. **Unbreakable employees know that the success of an organization is never reliant on only one person, but on group effort.** For example, they may be able to overcome obstacles and get crucial assistance through personal troubles that might otherwise have a detrimental impact on the workplace.

Being able to **successfully manage one's workload and cooperate with others** is an asset to any workplace that has unbreakable employees. The ability to bounce back from adversity and have a positive outlook on the future is one of the most important factors in increasing productivity.

Finally, unbreakable employees are more likely to adopt a **growth mindset,** which encourages them to actively seek out learning opportunities. A company's growth is accelerated when its people are eager to learn and develop their skills.

As a business owner, why is collaboration important for unbreakability?

We are living in a post pandemic world. The effects of the virus and the lasting troubles it has left us with have forced us to adapt to many changes, be it at home or in the workplace. I myself found things changing with the advent of work from home. Suddenly, work timelines were no longer between nine and six but from nine in the morning to nine at night. Hours doubled, work tripled—but I kept my strengths intact. As a manager, it is important to know how you can deal with challenging new situations and keep the morale of your team members high.

We must remember that we cannot always determine our circumstances, but we can certainly choose how we respond to them. With each problem that you face, try to look for solutions that will help you to never face the problem again instead of simply doing away with it for the time being. Look for lasting solutions—ones that leave an impact on both you and your company.

If you are an HR manager, it is important to focus on growth opportunities both at the individual employee and team levels so that as a whole, your company becomes more and more invincible. This is needed not just for supporting your staff, but also in developing a reputation as a powerful organization that attracts top talent.

Curiosity is a gift, so nurture it. Keep your organization diverse, for when you have a good mix of backgrounds and experiences, you also end up with a plethora of creative answers to choose from. You get the opportunity to learn from new people and their ways of handling different situations. Remember that every employee is intrinsically valuable, so appreciate and encourage the free flow of constructive feedback and opinions. Unbreakability is bound to happen when the team knows that they are gunning for a leader who has their backs—so always, always show support.

Be authentic in the vision and mission of your organization. Set goals, both short and long-term, and ensure that these goals are measurable and identifiable rather than abstract or lofty ideals. If you find that something is not going the way you expected, reach out and build a connection so that your teams and you can come to a constructive solution together.

The more divorced you are from your employees, the more disconnected your company philosophy will become. This leads to constant doubt and fear—*what happens next? What if the boss is unhappy? Are our jobs on the line?* These thoughts hamper the spirit of unbreakability, so try to ensure that they never arise in your employees' minds. And most importantly, always encourage open communication between your workers and the upper management. The more collaboration there is, the clearer things become. Everyone understands what is expected of them, and the possibility of miscommunication reduces drastically.

So, how do you build unbreakability? I'll say right off the bat that it isn't something you are born with, but rather something that you nurture.

How can you build unbreakability?

Little things that you do every day can be immensely impactful in terms of developing unbreakability, so let's take a look at a few of them.

First, **build good connections, or work at preserving the solid ones that you already have.** Good relationships take time, so if you have loving and genuine people in your life, prioritize the time and attention you invest in them. The more you connect with people, the greater their interest will be in your well-being as well as in knowing what keeps you grounded and stable. This knowledge gives you the room to grow while becoming unbreakable because the people who matter to you respect your needs and your space.

Work on emotional regulation and thought management. As much as you can, always keep your hopes up while being grounded in reality. Don't make daydreams out of your hopes—know that they are there to sustain you, but when working or doing something in real-time, keep your focus rooted. Accept that setbacks and transitions are perennial things in life and that your goals should not be predicated on them.

Grow self-love. This is easier said than done, but take care of your body and your mind. Eat properly, stay physically fit and upbeat, and try to keep away from toxic relationships and unhealthy coping systems. You are whole and wonderful, and you deserve an unadulterated life.

It is often difficult to plan for the future, which makes it all the more important for you to **treat each day with the best of your productive skills.** You may not always be able to plan long-term, so do what you do daily well. Take breaks in between work to spend some time out in nature. Connect with others and see where your common grounds lie. The more you spread yourself, the bigger your heart becomes—enabling you to see that life is best lived without crumbling at every corner.

Take the time to do things that mean something to you. In the context of your job, you may not always get to work on things you like or relate to—and that is true for all of us. So when you get the time, go out or stay in and do something that makes you truly happy. This can be painting, singing, writing, going to a shelter to volunteer, or anything else that uplifts you. This will not just build resilience, it will help you to ground yourself in reality with the understanding that what is real can also be beautiful.

Finally, **don't force it**. If you find that a particular situation is getting too out of hand or becoming too difficult, don't think that you *must* tough it out else everyone else will think less of you. *Do what feels right to you—unbreakability should never feel forced, it should come as a natural offshoot of your own beliefs and principles.* There are going to be exceptionally difficult days, and sometimes, you need to acknowledge the necessity of stepping back and taking a deep breath. But when you do come back, come back stronger.

In the end, unbreakability will be the judge of whether you are just getting by every day, or whether you are truly living and enjoying every second of your life. It will help you adapt to the stresses of changing times with a spirit that is tolerant and joyful. You will know that success will come to you eventually, even if it takes more than one try. With this in mind, let's take a look at the three core principles of unbreakability.

Principles of unbreakability

We may not know it, but each of us possesses the strength to be unbreakable even in the direst circumstances. This is mandated in the principles that make up the core of unbreakability.

The first principle is **adaptability.** There will always be those occasions when you plan something and things don't go the way you thought they would. You hope for a promotion or a reward at work and you are met with resistance. You study hard and don't see the results you expected. You work out for a month and find you've lost only two pounds. But is that the end of the road? *It doesn't have to be.* What of the journey that got you here? You learned so much about yourself in the process—especially how much you are capable of. That learning is immensely valuable, and if I may say so, the core of living life.

Adapt. Find other ways to work around situations, or take a deep breath and try again. Sometimes, things don't work out because we are meant for different things that are better for us. It just takes a bit of reorientation to understand and accept that. Work as you always would, with the same energy and motivation that you gave to your goal, but understand that your outcomes are not always linear—*but they will come.*

The second principle is **healing.** Recovering from disappointment can be very difficult, especially in situations of dire stress. All of us have burdens we carry, and sometimes the weight of these burdens can take months to shed. Unbreakability is knowing that you are bigger than the circumstances which try to break you. It is acknowledging that hurt is painful, but also that you have what it takes to survive and get on with life. The key to that is accepting the pain or anger or any other emotions you may be repressing, and to understand that it is normal to feel them. When you do that, you open the road to healing and recovery.

The final principle is **strength.** Often, we break down because of the difficulties of our circumstances, but there is always the option to stand back up. Retreat when things get out of hand, reassess your circumstances, and plan an outcome. This gives you the time to release pent-up emotions and tensions, and you come out of the stressful situation with more strength, absolutely indomitable and unbreakable. It will be easier to deal with difficulties that come later on if you've gone through this process. It's because you know for sure that you can make it through the ordeal. You have evidence that things will improve.

If you ask me, the most important thing in life is to find a balance. Just as fragility can sometimes make us hide from the truth, so also it can sometimes make it impossible for us to do anything that falls short of being perfect. We become too preoccupied with making things look good for others—with being proverbial superheroes who will always be there to save others' days even if our own is falling apart. Finding a balance ensures that you know when to work for others, and you know when you should be devoting time to yourself.

Within psychology, there's a concept called SPIRE—it breaks into Spirituality, Physical, Intelligence, Relational, and Emotional. At all times, try to ensure that your life is connected to all these elements. They are your core selves—the ways and frequency with which you connect to others, the physical work you do, the time you spend learning and acquiring new knowledge, the relationships you build, and your emotional health. Each of these traits is important and needs time and care.

So take time to empower yourself. That is very important because in empowering yourself, you empower those around you with the best of who you are and what you have to give. There are days you will find your natural self is at odds with the rest of the world— understand that this is normal and it is a time for you to step back and just be at peace with yourself. This will help you recenter your attention on the present and to know that no matter what, you will find the strength to come back all guns ablaze. Stay true to who you are, *because that is the most unbreakable skill in itself—it takes immense strength and power to know "this is me, and I will live to the best of my abilities and do what is expected of me within the boundaries of who I am."*

This, my friend, is finding a balance. Unbreakability thrives on it.

In the next chapter, we will discuss the importance of building positivity as a skill and how it will help you. Before that, let's sum up the key points of this chapter.

CHAPTER SUMMARY

- Unbreakability is a skill that can be learned.
- Unbreakability is a virtue that keeps you grounded and helps you deal with challenging situations.
- It is important for workspaces to develop unbreakability and resilience in employees as a way to generate collaborative effort and success.
- As a manager, allow open discussions and constructive feedback to help foster unbreakability in your employees.

- Take time out for yourself and set your boundaries.
- Foster good connections and be open to developing and adapting to changes.
- Find a balance in all that you do.
- Emotional regulation is a key way for you to achieve unbreakability.

3

POSITIVITY

> *"When things go wrong, don't go with them."*
>
> — ELVIS PRESLEY

P ositivity is one of the most important traits that will help you weather life's many storms. Maintaining a positive attitude isn't really about always smiling, it's about keeping an optimistic mindset and a hopeful attitude even if things may be in absolute chaotic conditions. Just like the difference between a bad and a good diet can break or build your body, the difference between a negative and positive mindset can be the very reason as to whether your life is mostly sunshine with a little rain or all rain.

The more you keep your eyes ahead and your spirits up, the more you will feel the power of gratitude and the ability to see that life is bigger than the harsh circumstances it sometimes brings. Thinking optimistically can clear your mind of many negative thoughts and allow you to feel grateful for the things you have. You stop thinking that you have always been disfavored or wallowing in self-pity, and you stop blaming others for your position and bearings in life. You will be able to command the flow of your emotions and find valuable learnings in every hardship that you encounter.

KICKING OFF NEGATIVITY

Kicking negativity from your life can be hard, especially if you have spent all your life feeling that things are not working out the way they are meant to. It is very easy to let toxicity take the upper hand in your life, more so because being positive takes time and work. However, once you get the hang of it, being positive will help you adopt good habits that will reduce toxic negativity and improve your quality of living. You can always use a few of these suggestions to make sure that you are trying to build positivity every day.

First, practice positive affirmations

An affirmation is a positive remark you repeat to your-self to help you combat and overcome self-defeating and self-destructive thought patterns. You may begin to see good changes in your life if you repeat and believe these mantras over and over again. Positive affirmations might be thought of as mental workouts, similar to the kind we do to enhance our physical health. Positive mental repetitions may rewire our brains, causing us to behave and think differently over time.

Affirmations can be effective in the treatment of mental health issues such as poor self-esteem, depression, and anxiety. This is because they trigger brain regions associated with making healthy lifestyle choices.

Affirmations may reduce stress, increase academic performance, reduce anxiety and fear, encourage individuals to adopt positive dietary and behavioral responses, and reduce resistance to changes—therefore helping us meet any challenges with ease. The benefits of affirmations don't end there; they also help us become more adaptable, elevate our souls, and heal our bodies. Affirmations may improve your job performance. Before a high-stakes meeting, try something next time—take five minutes to reflect on your finest attributes. You may find that this approach works wonders to reduce anxiety, boost self-esteem, and raise the likelihood of good outcomes. So, the next time you find a negative thought like, *"they have everything while I have nothing,"* consciously choose to change this pattern to thinking, *"I choose to achieve the things I want without comparing my life and timeline to that of others."*

Next, set goals that are achievable

Sometimes, we humans are creatures of lofty ambition —and don't get me wrong, there is absolutely nothing wrong with that. Problems arise when we set goals that far exceed our realistic capabilities at a given point in time. So, hypothetically let's say that we want to lose weight. We decide we want to aim for losing ten pounds in four days. For very obvious reasons, we cannot do it—and in the end, we are left feeling inadequate and frustrated.

On the other hand, if we choose goals that are specific, measurable, achievable, realistic and time-bound; we automatically set ourselves up for success. Instead of ten pounds, if we aim for one pound in four days which is far more realistic, we increase our chances of success and therefore, of obtaining a true and lasting sense of accomplishment that is instrumental in building positivity, helping us achieve our long-term goals, and fighting off negative influences.

Sleep properly, and without disturbances

There's a reason why so many of us wake up feeling tired, frustrated, and anxious when we sleep four hours a night. Our body has a natural circadian rhythm that dictates the flow of motions, and when we do not observe proper sleeping habits, we essentially compromise our body's ability to regulate essential functions with optimal ease.

Getting plentiful sleep is instrumental in fighting the effect of toxic negativity because it can improve your overall productivity and enhance concentration. Sleep deprivation leads to negative implications for your cognitive function, a fall in focus levels, and low productivity and performance. It can also negatively impact your emotions and ability to have proper social relationships—it's very difficult to not be in a bad mood all the time when you are stressed and tired! Poor sleeping patterns lead to the inability to understand crucial social information and cues—when you are rested, you become more aware of things happening around you and how you can process them.

Eat healthy food

It's no secret that eating healthy will leave you feeling upbeat all day because your body possesses the ability to recognize when you are doing something good for it.

Healthy food regulates your body functions and helps you maintain a good energy balance. Looking good has a lot to do with how you feel inside, and if your insides are burning up with acid reflux from your last greasy burger and fries—you won't be feeling that good outside. Focus on a balanced diet that emphasizes whole grains, protein, and healthy fats. Include green vegetables and healthy nuts and oils in your diet—these will also help fight fatigue and give you essential energy boosts. Overall, eating healthy will change how you feel about yourself, making you proud of the work you are putting in and therefore enhancing positivity.

Return some love to society at large

There's a plethora of research that says that when you give to others, you give back to yourself. Stephen Post, the author of *Why Good Things Happen to Good People*, writes that giving back to others has proven to increase health among victims of chronic diseases—including aids and multiple sclerosis (Marsh & Suttie, 2010). In 1999, a study found that older people who volunteered for two (or more) social organizations reportedly exhibited a 44% lesser chance to die over a five-year span than non-volunteers (even though the latter could exhibit other patterns of good health like good exercise habits, controlling practices like smoking and optimum general health.)

A 2003 study conducted by Stephanie Brown also displayed the same results with regard to elderly couples. Along with her colleagues, she found that individuals who extended help to their neighbors, relatives, and friends or provided emotional support to their spouses and families exhibited a lower risk of dying within a five-year period than those who did not (Marsh & Suttie, 2010). She also found that receiving help wasn't linked to a reduction in health risks— suggestive of the fact that giving back is more important and gratifying than receiving.

Giving may benefit physical health and lifespan in part because it reduces stress, which is linked to a number of health issues. Researchers from Johns Hopkins University and the University of Tennessee found that persons who offered positive reinforcement to others exhibited lower blood pressure than those who didn't, indicating that those who give of themselves experience greater physiological upliftment and overall positivity (Piferi & Lawler, 2006).

Meditate every day

Meditation is a wonderful means to establish a lasting connection between your body and your thoughts to consciously fight off negative influences from your life. It can ground you, help you turn your attention within yourself, and enable you to enter a state of deep relaxation. The more you consciously delve into your energies, the more you will get to the source of your negative thoughts, therefore getting the very real chance to cut off this source at its very origins. Conscious meditation is instrumental in staving off the pain, atypical depression, and anxiety.

Be grateful

Practicing gratitude for everything you have in your life is a great way to build more positivity. Gratefulness lies in acknowledging the impact of the positive things that are present in your life and in recognizing how they have made an impact on you. You can do this via thankfulness exercises, maintaining a gratitude journal, or by doing something as simple as letting a loved one know that you are grateful for their presence in your life. It is a beautiful way to be more optimistic and hopeful about your life and all the good things that it has brought your way.

Exercise

When you work out, your heart rate rises and your brain gets access to an increased flow of oxygen. Multiple studies have revealed that a well-oxygenated brain aids in the management of anxiety and depression, and this process may have an impact on your general mood (Mandolesi et al., 2018). Other research suggests that regular physical activity may help reduce symptoms of sadness and anxiety (*Hyperbaric Oxygen Therapy for Adults with Mental Illness: A Review of the Clinical Effectiveness*, 2014).

During exercise, your body produces additional mood-enhancing chemicals, such as serotonin and dopamine (Carek et al., 2011), that remain in your brain for a few hours afterward. Additionally, research suggests that your body produces chemicals called endorphins after twenty minutes to half an hour of aerobic activity (Mandolesi et al., 2018), which interact with receptors in the brain to lower your sense of pain.

Finally, do one thing at a time, and do it well

You may rid yourself of negativity by reducing your stress levels. Overcomplicating your life by attempting to do several things at once is a recipe for disaster. Focus on the work at hand and avoid distractions. Reducing distractions and creating a strategy for completing your activities one at a time is an option instead of attempting to do them all at once.

You may not quite be aware of this, but negative thoughts can be major dampeners, especially when it comes to maintaining your morale. They show up unexpectedly and carve a niche in your mind, becoming more and more pervasive—until a time comes when you cannot focus on anything because of how anxious and frustrated you feel. This is particularly true in the case of workplace toxicity—and with that, let's take a look at what happens when negativity pervades your work atmosphere.

NEGATIVITY KILLS YOUR WORKPLACE MORALE: AS A BOSS, HOW DO YOU FIX IT?

Negativity within a work environment can translate to poor overall performance and individual employee dissatisfaction, and feelings of severe inadequacy. Regardless of whether you are top management, the CEO themselves, or an employee, negativity hampers your company's reputation and has real consequences on each and everyone working for the company. In the long run, it can also hamper the company's ability to attract and retain a knowledgeable workforce.

The Society for Human Resource Management has reported that employees who have left their companies because of toxic company culture have cost organizations upwards of 220 billion dollars from 2015 to 2020 (Mirza, 2019). Additionally, the SHRM reports that 1/3rd of employees report that their managers actively participate in upholding a toxic work environment that doesn't leave any room for open or constructive dialogues.

About 1/4th feel that they don't get the respect they deserve. Gossip, conflicting issues, prejudiced management, workplace bullying, and lack of recognition all work to negatively influence employee retention, morale, and engagement. Anxiety, worry, and despair are all indications of job burnout, which may also produce physical symptoms like headaches and muscular discomfort. It's possible that these issues might have a negative impact on one's ability to perform at work, which could ultimately affect one's career.

These issues can cost your work environment by enticing deserving workers to leave for better places, and hurt your organization's bottom line (Menon & Priyadarshini, 2018). Within the organization, the pervasiveness of toxicity means that it can quickly spread from employee to employee, and if left unaddressed, it can impact the rates of productivity anywhere between 30-50%.

High employee turnover may also arise as a result of a toxic work environment. It may lead to litigation for harassment, discrimination, or libel in the worst-case situation. According to a study published in the International Journal of Environmental Research, high employee turnover and job unhappiness are linked to social exclusion at work. Employee productivity and well-being may be harmed as a result in the long term. Harassment, intimidation, and other forms of aggression can have harmful repercussions.

Almost everyone has had a bad experience at work at some time in their lives. It's possible that a member of your team spread gossip about a coworker or acted improperly toward a new employee. A lack of trust in one another, disagreement and failure to perform one's obligations may occur in the workplace. Consequently, your company will suffer financial losses and lose out on potential. The amount of complaints from customers is expected to rise as well. Your job as an owner/manager is to handle these issues before they get out of hand. These little concerns may contribute to workplace stress, a lack of cooperation, and a decrease in production.

In tandem, if employees are dissatisfied and unhappy with the state of affairs at work, they will likely carry the negativity they feel during office hours back home, affecting not just themselves but for all their loved ones. It is important to ensure that your employees feel appreciated and valued within their workspace not just for their mental health, but for the overall well-being of all those around them. A culture of positivity can help immensely when it comes to this. To build this culture,

you can follow some simple techniques. Let's take a
look at them:

- Try to locate the source of the negativity. Is it
  originating from upper management? Are the
  top-level employees not open to constructive
  conversations, open dialogue, or feedback?
  Does the office have a clear divide where there's
  unhealthy competition between the top
  management and the rest of the workforce? Is
  the opportunity for growth equal for everyone?
  Ask yourself all these important questions and
  try to find the answers. Once you get to the
  source of all issues, you will be able to find
  solutions.
- Show up at work, be accessible, and talk
  positively. When the boss is approachable and
  has a sunny disposition, it rubs off on all
  employees and makes them feel proud to be
  part of a work culture where the boss is
  motivating them to do their best every day. To
  make the best workspace, it is always
  imperative to lead by example.
- Be flexible and transparent in your approaches.
  If your employees truly feel that their voices are
  heard and that each of them is contributing

something valuable to the work environment, chances are that they will experience job satisfaction. Leave room for communication and allow for constructive opinion generation and feedback without letting anyone walk over you—the idea is to listen to all suggestions and put into effect those which will benefit your organization, irrespective of whether they come from the lower-level employees or the top management.

- Have a concrete understanding of the company's core values and the main product that you represent. If the very idea that you are working towards is something abstract and falls out of your level of understanding, how can you expect your workforce to relate to it? Nothing dampens morale like the idea of working for something that you cannot relate to or have no understanding of, and on top of that, if your employees feel that you are as disconnected as them, their desire to relate to the product or vision decreases further. So, take time to understand the core organizational principles and ensure that they are shared during collaborative meetings in as lucid a manner as possible.

- Finally, leave room for enjoyment too—nobody likes to feel like they are being worked to their death. Hold office lunches, coffee breaks, joint sessions for brainstorming, and the opportunity for your employees to have little corners in the office where they can let their creativity shine. This can be instrumental in making them feel like they really matter within the workspace, resulting in a positive, upbeat workforce that is committed to your organization and you.

As people, we spend almost all of our lives worrying about the things that might or might not happen in the future.

PESSIMISM, OPTIMISM, AND REALISM: THE BALANCE LIES IN-BETWEEN

I speak from personal experience when I tell you that I spent years worrying about the what-ifs.

Will we get married? Will our children grow up to be capable adults? Will we have enough money to travel the world? Will the stock market fall once again? Will the dollar retain its hold, or will we experience inflation? Will I ever be healthy?

There's so much riding on this "will"—one thought after another spent on the expectation and fear of things that may or may not come to fruition. In all these cases, we are trying to give a body to our future (or our expectations of the future). The issue is that nobody can exactly say what the future will hold for us. Just as some things are predictable constants, so also other things can change and transform in a matter of seconds. Now, most of us tend to be optimistic in our hopes for what the future will hold. We believe that we will have good lives and add more value to our existence, so we invest and open savings accounts and ensure that our children attend good schools. The expectation is that since we are putting value into something right now, this value will increase and contribute to our peace of mind ten years down the line.

On the other hand, some of us can be pessimistic about the future—always worrying that life is out to get us with talons and claws, always fearing that the worst is just about to happen, and therefore planning to ensure we stay safe. Those of us who are too afraid to commit, settle, live happily in the present, and find joy in the little things tend to belong to this group.

If you'd ask me, I'd say that neither is sustainable in the long term. I'd prefer a middle ground, or in other words, to ensure that I remain positive in spite of what circumstances I am presented with, I choose to be a *realist*. Simply speaking, rather than always worrying that the worst is out to get me or always living under the stress of expecting to be rewarded with the very best that life has to offer, I choose to ask myself—*"If I am presented with a worst-case scenario, do I have the resources I need to get through it and keep living life?"*

And if something unexpectedly good happens, I choose to be grateful for it, with the knowledge that life will not always be so predictably good or *safe.* This means that while I appreciate the goodness that has been given to me in the present moment, I also choose to *enjoy it in the present moment rather than constantly focusing on when another event of equal magnitude will occur.*

Being a realist means that you keep your focus on the things that actually happen—and on finding solutions to tackle them. This doesn't mean that you stop planning for the future altogether. It means that you plan ahead, but with the sound knowledge that everything may not go according to plan, and the faith that you have what it takes to get through unforeseen circumstances.

Let's face it, life likes to surprise us from time to time, and if we aren't open to unexpected turns, the only results we are left with are broken minds and exhausted hearts. Instead, you choose to do everything you can *in the present moment* that will maximize a sense of contentment with what you have, while also setting you up for a stable future (regardless of the turns it may take).

To put it another way, being a realist is a combination of both pessimism and optimism—a kind of middle ground between the two. You begin as a pessimist, looking out for things that may go awry and preparing yourself to handle them. Once you've taken care of the foreseeable things that may go wrong, you lean on optimism to enhance the opportunities to enable good things to come to you. What you need is a balance between the core principles of pessimism and those of optimism—essentially, you engender optimism by cultivating early pessimism to your advantage.

Plenty of events that will happen in the course of our lives are outside the realms of our control—but this doesn't mean that we need to lock ourselves in our rooms and spend the rest of our lives in the dark. It also doesn't mean that we internalize the thought that only bad things will ever happen to us. Because, *bad things happen to everybody—and this is just one of life's eventualities, regardless of whether you are a daily wage earner or born a billionaire.* Yes, the circumstances will be different—but who are we to judge what the definitions of "bad things" are for different people and to blame our fortunes for the things that happen?

What we can do instead is focus on the root cause of our issues—and to handle them as best as we can. For example, if our issues are stemming from a lack of finances, we plan ahead by investing in a health emergencies fund, keeping a store of essentials like basic food and drink, and spending reasonably so that we don't incur mammoth debts. Other concerns include planning ahead for health and life insurance, some thoughts as to how we want to live after retirement, and whether we want to make a will. These are the very basics, but once you have these sorted, you know that your basic finances are in order—so much so that a financial crisis tomorrow will not affect you majorly, and you will be able to survive through it.

Similarly, other investments you need are your time, critical thinking, and energy. Eat healthy for basic well-being, exercise for mental and physical fitness, and mix with positive people so that your life doesn't become a toxic modernist impression of *La Mélancolie*. Practice good hygiene, take time to hone your creative skills, and spend enough time with yourself. These are the things within your control, and you can choose to be the very best in each of them, or not. If you are, you automatically make room for protecting yourself from most of life's storms and ensuring that you have the resources you need to make it through each of them.

Summing up, what I'm saying is that *you have the power to choose balance. That is what realism is.* It is the knowledge that some events will always be out of our control, but we do have the resources to ensure that we can survive through these events and emerge with greater wisdom. That is the ultimate definition of positive living.

It isn't inherently bad to be a core pessimist or a core optimist—but being a realist means that you give yourself the opportunity to experience the best of optimism while using pessimism to *ensure your safety.* After all, we are creatures who thrive on predictability, even those among us who profess to experience the thrill in the unexpected. When you choose realism, you choose to find positivity in your daily existence, irrespective of what events come your way. What more could one ask for?

Perhaps one of the hardest things you will learn in this life is to hold on to hope in tough situations. This is not easy—it requires you to understand that no matter how tough situations get, you will be tougher. We often find it easier to place that hope in others, because if things don't work out according to our expectations, laying the blame on others is simpler than really looking within to see what went wrong, addressing it, and readjusting our expectations. But believe me, in all that the world is and all that it has to offer, hope is the one thing that will carry you through all trials and tribulations.

HOW DO YOU KEEP HOPE ALIVE?

You've just received the news that the promotion you worked all year for is going to someone else. The increment you wanted will take another year. The trip you were waiting all year for got canceled due to some inexplicable reasons. The relationship you have learned to depend on is growing sour. The results you expected fall far short of how hard you studied.

We've all been there. The darkness that eclipses our lives after being let down—especially when we cannot look to anyone else except ourselves. So, what can you do to keep hope alive, irrespective of how despondent the situation feels?

Well, little things, and one step at a time. Let's take a look.

Express what you feel

When we are experiencing a major setback or an unprecedented loss, some of us think that the way forward is to repress our feelings and push through. The notion that this is showing strength is wrong— because you are actually being fragile. Strength lies in *acknowledging the effect of this loss, in feeling what it makes you feel, and in finding ways to move ahead with the learning that it brings to you.*

Try to talk about things with someone who is close to you or write your feelings in a diary or journal. Release the tide of negative emotions that are in your soul, and that is interfering with your hope that things will get better. When negative emotions arise, don't waste precious time judging yourself or feeling that they make you weak—they don't. They are natural, everyone has them, and weakness is subjective. What matters is using each setback as a lesson, and this can only be done when you express how the setback made you feel.

Never lose hope in... hope

Look for hope in everyday mundane things. Have you ever seen that the smallest of things have given rise to some form of joy? The little spark of happiness you feel when you sip on a cup of hot tea. The friend you talk to after years apart from each other. The special dish cooked for you by your spouse or family member. The little conversation you have with a loved one after a long and tiring day at work. Take a look around you, and be present in the little joys of life that envelop your existence. Make this part of your everyday routine— you may be surprised at how unexpectedly hope turns up.

Keep your eyes on the possibilities

In times of despair, seeing a brighter future might give you the motivation to seek out solutions. The creation of a clear strategic direction, which is a distinct mental image of the intended goal might assist you with this process. You must be motivated and empowered to pursue your goal, no matter what hurdles are thrown at you. A compelling vision may be, for example, to work on a passion project, publish a book on a subject you are passionate about, go on a hard-earned trip, or establish a company. Imagining what you want to achieve gives you hope.

Don't compete, learn

Don't waste your time worrying about what other people have that you lack. It is because of your uniqueness that you are important. Instead of comparing yourself to others, seek those that challenge or motivate you to improve. In a completely new environment, we may learn so much from one another and discover new facets of ourselves. Consider putting yourself in a position where you can learn from individuals you would consider to be your competition. Remember that every new encounter brings with it the opportunity to learn something important about yourself and the world around you—so approach that with full gusto.

Be grateful

Practicing appreciation, no matter how trite it may seem, might help you feel more positive. When you focus on all the things you have to be thankful for, you get a new sense of well-being and a more positive outlook on life. Gratitude may be cultivated by keeping a gratitude book where you write down two to six things a day for which you are thankful. Alternatively, you might begin or finish your day by thinking of something for which you are thankful.

Spend time outdoors

Hope is in the way nature works. Plants are born, old trees wither, seasons change, and life moves on. Also, a new day provides us with an opportunity for a fresh start, to rectify things, and speak what's on our minds. It's hard to think of a better approach to cultivate optimism than to get up every day and take in the beauty of creation. Merely walking outdoors on a winter morning, feeling the crispy crunch of autumn leaves beneath your boots, basking in the gentle warmth of the early sun—the little pleasures that cost nothing—can teach you to be joyful because you are living in such a beautiful world.

Be good to others

Kindness is key to building hope. It can be as simple as visiting a shelter to show some love to animals in need, sharing a good meal with friends and family, doing volunteer work, or calling up a friend who is going through a tough time. You don't need to be a millionaire to partake in charity—indeed, the greatest acts of kindness come from a charitable heart, not a charitable wallet. The mere feeling of *wanting to do good for others* can make a world of difference. Anything you do instills hope in the person at the receiving end and makes you feel uplifted.

Take care of yourself

It's difficult to love ourselves at any time, but it's extremely difficult to do so when things are tough. The loss of something that mattered to us has the ability to deflate our self-belief completely. We may point the finger at ourselves if we committed a mistake that resulted in an undesirable event. This is the time when we need to be most self-aware.

For example, you may improve your negative self-talk by being more aware of the root causes of it. Whenever you catch yourself using a phrase like *"I'm no good at this,"* correct yourself by saying *"I choose to take time to hone this strength."* Eat right, spend time doing physical activities, and always know that you are enough—the world is a big place, and there is room for everyone. Imagine the life you desire and commit to making it a reality, which is likely to inspire you.

Build faith

Faith connects with us on a very deep level, as we all know. It is a proclamation of faith and hope that extends beyond the conscious mind. Everything we hold dear is based on a foundation of faith and optimism. For a person to be uplifted, they must have trust and hope in the same thing. Everyone, regardless of their circumstances, needs to have hope.

Everyone has to have faith in order to embrace the promises of hope that are made. It is difficult to have either hope or faith if the other does not exist first. Having faith strengthens the conviction that, after asserting a claim to something, we can attain it provided we remain focused on the end objective and take constant activity. That is all that is required at times.

Grow spirituality

Spirituality is not the same as being religious. It is finding a way to connect deeply with yourself and the world around you. The more you hone spirituality, the better you know yourself. This is intrinsic in developing an instinctive knowledge of the things you value, what makes you happy and what makes you "unique" and a whole, complete individual who is capable of anything they set their mind to. You may also discover previous beliefs that are preventing you from achieving your goals. Having access to this inner knowledge provides hope for a brighter future.

You have the power to choose how you respond to your current situation and how you will respond to what comes ahead if you choose to hope. Maintaining a positive perspective through difficult times might be difficult, but remember that you can always rely on hope to view things in a fresh light.

If you have been made to believe that hopeful people live with their heads in the clouds—I'll take a minute to correct this notion. Hopeful people do not simply dream—they imagine what their futures will look like and act upon them. They make measurable and achievable goals and short-term plans that will help them reach these goals. Most of all, they build faith in their capacity to achieve the visions that matter to them, while recognizing that they may encounter stress, failure, and many bitter lessons along the way.

Hope is a choice. You choose to cultivate it. It makes you adaptive. It teaches you that even if you may fail sometimes, you can reorient and find other ways to obtain the outcomes you want.

Hope rests on one's conviction that one can attain one's objectives. *And this is where it is connected to mental strength—in the belief that you do have what it takes, and in putting all of yourself into achieving it.* Remember when we said that grit is the most important trait you can develop when it comes to achieving success? Well, hope is grit's shadow, constantly telling you that you are enough, that *you will always be enough.*

In the next chapter, we will talk about the skill of *commitment,* and how it can help you get through life's tough situations. Before we go there, let's take a minute to sum up the key points of this chapter.

CHAPTER SUMMARY

- When it comes to maintaining a good attitude, it isn't really about constantly smiling; rather, it is about maintaining optimistic thinking and a hopeful outlook even when everything is in utter chaos.
- Practicing spirituality is a good way to connect with yourself and to grow more hope.
- Positivity teaches us that life is beautiful and we should spend time enjoying it and living it fully.

- It is possible to eliminate negativity from your life by engaging in activities such as positive affirmations, making measurable objectives, eating nutritious foods, participating in volunteer work, and being appreciative.
- Because a negative work environment may have a negative impact on productivity and production, if you are a business owner, you should make sure that your staff feels valued.
- Ensure that as a company owner, you have a clear idea of the organizational visions and knowledge of the end product.
- It is critical to undertake one task at a time in order to avoid being overburdened with work.
- Practice giving to others in little ways to fulfill yourself.
- By embracing reality, you may achieve a healthy balance between pessimism and optimism.
- Always have confidence in hope, since it will teach you how to withstand the storms of life.

4

COMMITMENT

> *"There's a difference between interest and commitment. When you're interested in something, you do it only when circumstances permit. When you're committed to something, you accept no excuses, only results."*
>
> — ART TUROCK

S o, you have made a plan to get your life in order. You wake up feeling a sense of renewed purpose. You feel that nothing can stop you now—no matter what, you are going to get to your goals and clear all hurdles that try to thwart your progress. Then, one hurdle actually comes your way. And you give up immediately because you think that it's too difficult, you cannot find the resources or motivation you need to continue, it's just easier to stay in bed and daydream. Dear readers, if this is something you conform to (and trust me, I've been there) then a time will come when you will wake up and look at life with great regret. The years will simply pass you by, and you'll wonder why you never really lived.

That is where commitment comes in. Commitment to something, anything that you set your mind to, is the only way to ensure that you stick to and fulfill your goals, regardless of how dire the circumstances may become. You know that the goal is your priority, and you have full-fledged faith in seeing it through. Regardless of how difficult the journey may be, your vision remains centered and your work remains steady. Commitment ensures that irrespective of the odds, you stick to the promises you make to yourself and to others.

HOW DO YOU STICK TO YOUR PLANS?

The first step towards achieving a concrete goal is to make a plan on how you will go about doing it. This plan should be specific to your situation and the visions you have—perhaps you want to lose weight? Perhaps you want to work on an important project and knock it out of the park? Perhaps you want to help your child do well in their exams? Whatever the goal is, making a plan will ensure that you have the basic steps down.

The more measurable and achievable your plan is, the easier it will be for you to work through any inconsistencies. This being said, while sticking to a plan is important, ensure that you leave room for any adjustments because life never follows a linear pattern. Your plan should be vital and ever-adaptive—what should remain intact is the end goal that the plan will help you to achieve.

Following through with the plans you make is where commitment comes in—and there are some little tips you can heed to ensure that things flow as smoothly as is possible.

Make SMART Plans

When writing the plans that will help you to achieve a goal, ensure that your plan follows the dictates of SMART planning—which means that you choose plans that are specific, measurable, achievable, realistic, and time-bound. The timeframe is more of something to aspire towards—don't let it become the priority. What's more important is for you to choose something that you can measure and observe, because abstract plans are really difficult to achieve. If you make a plan like "I want to become healthy," you yourself will get confused with the nitty-gritty like—*how do you become healthy? What does it entail? Where do you begin? What obstacles would you face? Do you have all the resources?* A better way to word this plan would be to say, *"I want to lose ten pounds in the next thirty days by doing cardio exercises and doing intermittent fasting."* This gives you a very real measure of what you want, how you will go about getting it, and within what time frame.

Write them down

Once you have your plan in place, write down all the steps you need to act upon to bring it to fruition. Use a journal or simply jot it down in a notepad or on your laptop—but make sure to get a print and stick it somewhere you can see it every day, like the surface of your refrigerator or on the cupboard. Make little notes of your progress once every two days. This visual will remind you why you are working so hard, and whenever temptations come your way, you will be able to look at the sheet and remember how hard you have worked to get to where you are, ensuring that you stay true to yourself and your input.

Set deadlines for yourself

Within a big plan, make little plans that will be a measure of your progress. Then, set different timelines for each of these plans. The shorter ones should take you anywhere between four days to a week, while the longer ones can take anywhere between a month to six. As time passes, you will be able to see how many plans you are completing and whether you are on track to get to the end goal as planned. However, make room for any unprecedented circumstances, and if you need to reorient or change any time-frames because of these circumstances, make sure that you remain adaptable. The timelines are simply there to help you measure progress.

Don't forget to reward yourself.

Go on movie dates with yourself. Cook wonderful meals or eat at a good restaurant once a month. Read a great book. Remember to pat yourself on the back every now and then because *you are working so hard and if you don't appreciate the effort you are putting in to become a better version of yourself, who will?*

Working towards your goals takes a lot of effort—and each time you accomplish something, show yourself the love and respect you deserve. On the other end, if you find that something hasn't quite worked out the way you planned, be compassionate to your soul. It's never the end of the road, and if you are kind to yourself, you'll notice many alternative routes come up that will help you to get to the ultimate end that you desire.

Get a partner

Are you planning to go on a diet, work out every day, or do something that can also be done in collaboration? Involve a friend or a close family member as an accountability partner—and you'll find that it works wonders for you when you try to achieve something. None of us like to feel that we are doing something alone, and company always has the advantage of making us understand that someone else is going through the same struggles as us. This gives our confidence levels a boost and can work wonders for achieving goals. The people who help you stick to your plans will show you what it means to stay committed in the long run—they will remind you of deadlines and encourage you whenever something gets in the way. So, find yourself someone who will help you be accountable to yourself.

You may be familiar with the term "commitment issues." What does it mean, though? In my experience, I have seen that commitment either is, or isn't. And in the case of the latter, a number of issues can be at fault.

THE ENEMIES OF COMMITMENT

Commitment issues or commitment phobia represent each circumstance where you feel a strong resistance when it comes to dedicating yourself to achieving a long-term goal. This can be sustaining a relationship, working for a promotion, sticking to one career path, or committing to long-term health. It's not that you don't want to, you *just don't feel the long-term energy or motivation that you need to sustain what you begin.* Problems with commitment could appear as a partner refusing to seek a greater degree of engagement in the relationship, such as tying the knot or shifting together.

Commitment concerns may seem as having a good time together but noting the other person is hesitant to progress to the next level of dating seriously to those just familiarizing with someone in the initial dating period. Or, it could be a whole different thing. It could be that you begin a process of losing weight, but as soon as you see that it is taking more time than expected, you give up. It can be that you take up the job you have always wanted, but you see that there's a lot of hard work involved in making a passion a reality, and you don't have the motivation or drive that this entails.

People who are devoted to a person, idea, or action are known as "committed." For some monogamous relationships or in the case of really wanting something and knowing you have what it takes to get it, commitment implies that you're prepared to go through the ups and downs together. One gets the impression of the development. A person with attachment issues, on the other hand, finds it difficult to feel committed and to go forward.

So, how do you know when commitment issues are rearing their ugly heads, and more importantly, how do you deal with them? Before going there, let's look at some of the reasons why commitment issues surface in the first place.

Many of us go in expecting to fail

We have a latent but looming fear that a good relationship will end unexpectedly, that we will always be second, or that we'll never get to that state of progression which we desire. This is more pronounced if we have known failure as a shadow—and the whole process of learning that failure is just a stepping stone to success can take time and relearning.

We worry that we have chosen the "wrong" goal/relationship/plan

This is flaky behavior, and all of us have experienced it at varying levels during the course of our lives. We take up a goal and decide that it's what we want, then we see or encounter another plan and think that it looks more attractive than ours. This makes us doubt our progress and the very notion of knowing what is best for us. We begin to measure our own progress based on how others are living their lives. The grass truly feels greener on the other side, and we become resentful and give up before taking our plan to a stage of fruition.

We become afraid of unhealthy decisions

Sometimes, we become so carried away by the impact of a plan, a relationship, or a goal, that a time comes when the very idea of it begins to scare us. The notions that some aspects will always be unknown, that the future remains unpredictable regardless of how hard we work, and that we may get hurt even if we go in with the best of intentions can thwart the most stable among us.

We have trust issues

This is truer when it comes to committing in a relationship. For some of us, the loss of confidence in someone close to us makes it difficult to trust anybody else in the future, even our spouses. We subconsciously begin to feel that we are incapable of being loved, and we transfer the worst-case scenario onto our prospective romantic partner, which might be disastrous.

We have attachment issues arising from childhood trauma

At any moment, repressed trauma and maltreatment may resurface, especially for those of us who have faced it constantly in the past. What arises from this is a severe lack of self-confidence. It resembles a sore. Because of this, even when you really want to heal, being with another person might be a persistent trigger and resurfacing of the wound. Our main providers are tasked with providing for our basic requirements and assisting us in acclimating to our new surroundings. A lack of care and attention as a child may become manifested in emotional insecurity as an adult, propelling us towards inconsistencies in relationships and in every task that we undertake.

Family dynamics is contributive to this, especially if we have been taught to live and act a certain way that is no longer in tandem with the things we want from life. Case in point, I have a friend whose family believed in greasy meals a day in and out. The bigger and oilier, the better. My friend grew up as obese as the others in his family, until the day he had a heart attack at the age of thirty. This brought him to his senses and he decided to work on bettering his health. At this stage, it's truly easier said than done, because the effort needs to be double-sided. You're not only learning new and better habits, but *you also have to unlearn everything that you have grown up with.*

With this, let's look at the different signs through which commitment issues can expose themselves:

- You're consciously avoiding thinking of the future. You know that you want to make a plan, and you may even have an idea of what you want out of this, but you are too afraid to go a few days ahead of today.
- You're okay with doing something today, but whenever you have to plan long-term you say something evasive like "let's see how it goes" because you are not comfortable with the very thought of investing in something on a long-term basis.
- You constantly self-sabotage. In the context of self-destructive activity, the phrase "self-sabotage" may be employed to mean situations where you are thwarting your own progress. You may not even recognize you're doing it at first. It's a type of psychological self-harm when bad habits undermine your efforts over time.

Self-defeating tendencies are as diverse as the people who have them. However, there are a few cases that keep coming up again and again. It is possible to "skip" a deadline or not prepare a presentation correctly because you're already convinced you'll fail. Maybe you're always running late for a meeting. You may procrastinate, putting off tasks that you know you must do. Self-sabotage shows up in a hundred different ways, and it can erode your chances at a good future and undermine your self-confidence to a very real extent.

You may begin tasks but fail to complete them. Even when provided with a wonderful chance, you are unable to go forward. It's also possible that you have grand plans for something that will have a lasting impact on your life, but you never act on them.

- You consciously avoid planning for the future because you are too afraid of things "feeling too real." Making plans causes you stress and anxiety. Instead of really working through things, you're content to leave your decisions to the wheels of time—and you often end up canceling plans and flaking on others.
- You spend hours questioning whether the plan or goal or relationship is really worth it. Sometimes, the amount of time you invest in questioning the worthiness of the goal or the relationship is more than the work you actually put in.

Usually, this is a sign that you are looking for little ways to know that the plan or the relationship won't work out, and the moment you have even a small inkling that something is inconsistent, it becomes a ground for you to think you were right and to walk out on the goal or the relationship without any further thought.

- You avoid serious relationships. Having a fear of commitment doesn't always indicate that you're promiscuous. Problems might arise if, for reasons you do not fully understand, you feel the urge to put a stop to things rather than allow them to evolve. This may not just be a part of your relationships, but can instead extend to all parts of your life.
- The very notion of "the next step" sends you into a nervous fit. If you are in a relationship and your partner wants to think ahead (which is natural in all healthy relationships) you feel like they are trapping you.

Any signs of deep love or affection or trust make you feel nervous and claustrophobic—and you keep thinking of wanting to escape. While the words themselves may validate you and make you feel important, you think that you're just not ready. And much like how it happens in relationships, this can extend to other parts of your life, where every time you see chances of something really happening, you back away because you are too scared of stabilizing yourself or sticking to something.

- You are always detached in your relationships, and you don't feel any sense of passion or being truly invested in the work that you are doing. You're just doing it for the heck of it, because someone told you to, or because it feels like the "normal thing to do." But inside, you can't relate to what is happening or what you are engaging in, and it all feels very alien. When you have no passion or love for what you are doing or who you are with, the moment an issue comes up, you may not think twice before packing your bags—which is a very real sign of commitment phobia.
- You find it difficult to stay in one job for more than a few months to a year. Whenever a slight hurdle comes your way, you find yourself looking for alternatives because starting all over feels easier than having to get through the hurdles.

Unfortunately, hurdles are a part of life, and you soon find the same kind of issues within your new workspace, and what happens is an endless stream of hopping from one job to the next, until a day comes when success feels as elusive as Eldorado.

- Finally, you consciously avoid all team-building and collaborative activities. Even if you're enthusiastic about a cause, it's possible that commitment issues are to blame for your lack of involvement in it. If you don't want to engage with your teammates outside of what is routine and compulsory, this might be an indication that you are finding it difficult to be committed to your career, or to any other aspect of life that runs on collaboration and teamwork. The desire to run alone can often give rise to escapism and the urge to avoid all responsibilities, both of which are real signs of commitment phobia.

Do you know what I truly believe? I have often heard that whenever people give up when the going gets tough, they say things like *"It just didn't feel good anymore," "I didn't have what it took," "It didn't feel like it was meant to be,"* or *"It didn't excite me anymore."* What's important here is that people often skirt around commitment by thinking that whenever things demand responsibility or time or real work, they get in the way of "being fun"—which becomes a plausible ground to stop trying.

The simple thing here is a *dire lack of belief.* We stop believing in our capabilities and consciously look for excuses to skirt around our responsibilities. What's worth noting is that if our minds believe that we can do it, we can. When you believe that you will fulfill a goal or a plan, you will end up building the circumstances that ensure you live up to the work needed to make the plan a reality. And, if you believe that "it just isn't worth it" every time something becomes difficult, you automatically make room for circumstances that entice you to give up. You look for little faults and small inconsistencies and blow them out of proportion until you can easily convince yourself that "it just isn't right for me."

Well, this just won't do, will it? No successful narrative comes on a bed of soft lilies and cashmere. There is no easy route to success, especially the lasting kind. Hard effort, discipline, persistence, tenacity, willpower, bravery and faith are all necessary for success. Here are some pointers to help you stick to your objectives, no matter what happens along the way:

- Create small but successful habits that you can
  practice every day. All the little things you do
  on a daily basis make up your habits. As simple

as drinking a glass of water when you wake up, eating a good breakfast, or going to work out at the same time each day. You may not understand the impact of these tiny routines on a day-to-day basis—but think of how they define your life in the long run! If you were to stop brushing your teeth for six months, how would you feel? If you stopped eating breakfast or drank cream-and-sugar laden coffee in the morning instead of water, do you think your body would be as grateful? Going to the gym on a regular basis has the same effect. You'll be disappointed if you anticipate results in the first week.

However, if you stick to your workout routine for six months, you'll certainly notice some progress and be nearer to your main intention. The advantage of small habits is that they may be carried out every day with little effort on your part. Every day, you should engage in your new routine so that it becomes a habit and you won't be tempted to put it off for the following day— and this will prepare you for bigger challenges along the way.

- Be responsible and accountable to someone else. You can make headway toward any of your objectives if you have a strong accountability partner. When things go wrong, it's frequently simpler to point the finger at someone else or something else in your life. Having an accountability partner who understands your goals and intentions may help you detect the moments when you lose focus—for they will ensure that you turn your attention inward rather than blaming the world.

A good friend or mentor may be a continual source of inspiration and encouragement to recharge your motivations when they begin to fail. A good accountability partner can help you keep track of your progress since they are a neutral observer of what you are working on. They may also aid in the discovery of your own assets and liabilities—and if they are invested in your success, they will know when they see inconsistencies that don't catch your immediate attention and tell you about the same.

You are able to acquire the support and guidance you need to identify behaviors that might threaten your progress and gradually break undesirable habits. As a result, you have a greater grasp of your own actions, ideas, and feelings. Achieving your objectives is easier when you're armed with the right tools—and sometimes, a person who acts as a mirror can be an amazing source of self-directed knowledge.

- Be proud of your small achievements. Anything you do that is in line with your goals is considered a "little victory." A regimen of self-criticism and rigidity may make it easy to overlook the little victories in life.

Let's assume that one of your aims is to be nice to other people. So, whenever you find someone struggling with spoken English, instead of judging them, you give them the due respect they are entitled to because just as they may not be adept at your mother tongue, so also you are not adept at theirs. You'll have a positive self-perception as a consequence, and it may lead to a great deal of contentment. Paying attention to your ideas allows you to examine the absurdity of making inappropriate distinctions based on dialect.

We experience a feeling of pride when we achieve something because it stimulates the reward region of our brains. As a result, the brain chemical dopamine is produced, causing us to feel happy. With the aid of this neurotransmitter, you might feel like you've been recognized and rewarded, which can lead to an increased desire to work more. As the saying goes, awareness is the prerequisite for effective life changes—

and isn't this just another form of consciousness? All you need are the little things to believe you are capable of big wins. Habits as small as making your bed when you get up, taking a walk in the morning, preparing a healthy meal, or saying a little prayer before you begin your day—each of these are tiny accomplishments of their own, and ones that you should feel proud to be doing.

- Finally, be unrelenting in the pursuit of your goals. The mark of successful people is an infallible belief in themselves. They remain in steady pursuit of the goals they believe in, regardless of setbacks or troubles along the way. They learn from the issues they encounter, pick themselves up, and carry forward with the new learnings. This is what makes someone successful—not the conviction that they cannot fail, but in trying over and again until they get to their end goal.

Develop an inner resolve that feeds you with all the good things that will happen once you achieve your goal—all the reasons why you are doing it in the first place. These thoughts will cancel out negative misbeliefs and keep you gunning for the only thing that matters—the vision you cherish in your heart.

Now, it can be that giving up before the finish line is in sight is just something you are used to doing. Subconsciously, you may even be aware of how your indecisiveness and lack of commitment have wreaked havoc in your personal and professional life.

BREAKING A HISTORY OF LACK OF COMMITMENT

Each and every goal, even the most rudimentary of them, requires a level of commitment. Every day, you wake up *choosing* to accomplish certain goals. You choose to drink water over sugary beverages. You choose to take a walk rather than getting up at ten and rushing to the office. You choose to have a healthy breakfast instead of a power bar and a bag of chips.

Each second, each moment of your life is the sum of the many little choices you make and your commitment to each of these choices. As a matter of fact, everything you have acquired in your life is the result of choosing to be committed to it—whether it is a new job or academic success, or good family dynamics.

The issue here is not with forming a commitment, but in finding ways to *stick with it.* Every time you make a commitment and go back on it, you are not only breaking the faith of others but eroding your own self-confidence. So, how can you ensure that your commitment levels stay high and that you remain dedicated to your causes?

Rather than showing involvement, show commitment

Of course being involved is wonderful, but it is also more transient. It means that you are interested in an aspect of what is going on and therefore investing yourself in it for the time being. When you are committed, you are investing yourself in one whole end, not the sum total of the parts that seem "interesting" irrespective of how relevant or irrelevant they are to this end. Being involved isn't a show of commitment, although being committed certainly encapsulates being involved. Simply speaking, when you are committed to something, you will be wholly involved in it, even in the parts which are the most uninteresting and tiresome. You won't back out because you know that this cause is something dear to your heart.

Make goals and revisit them as regularly as you can

Setting objectives helps you develop new habits, prioritize, and maintain your life momentum. Without objectives, we lose time, energy, and effort. Talent is vital, but frequently what you do with it determines your success. And how you use your gift relies on your goals which provide you with direction and focus to orient your talents. This mental focus can help you achieve your life objectives rather than just meandering around. Your attitudes and behaviors will be guided by these goals.

While setting goals, remember that they don't have to have be-all, end-all approaches. You need to revisit the objectives you set and the set of tasks you've laid out to get to these objectives from time to time. This will help you measure your progress, know whether you can ramp things up or whether you need to give yourself more time, and most importantly, whether the approaches you have chosen are the right fit for you, or whether you need to reorient them.

Don't be afraid of making mistakes

As a matter of fact, accept the very notion of mistakes happening as a given—because if the way forward is all smooth sailing, *how will you learn anything new?* There are going to be setbacks and problems along the way, and the more you adapt and learn, the more intelligent and capable you will become.

In the process of achieving your goals, you will find that your worst enemies are fear of commitment, lack of faith, and perfectionism. Do not prescribe to any of these—and remember that life itself is the sum total of

144 | EDRIC SCHUMAN

things you learn along the way. Perfectionism breeds rigidity and blinds you to the notion of learning from the world around you. That is no way to exist. And faith is something that will bolster your hope every day, so if you find yourself lacking it, do little exercises that will help you build more faith, not just in others, but also in yourself and in the bigger world around you.

Seek inspiration

One of the top reasons why we fail our commitments is our inability to stay inspired in the long run. We begin all guns blazing, find that our inspiration is dwindling, and give up. To prevent this from happening, look to people and things that inspire you—even the smallest and most obscure ones. If you draw inspiration from nature and the way life works outside of you, so be it. It doesn't have to come from a person, so long as you feel a sense of wanting to emulate them and what they stand for, anything works.

Even a bird hunting a safe ground to build a nest hours at an end, the way a tree survives a storm, or the ridiculous joy a child feels when you hand them a piece of sticky toffee can bring you inspiration. Embrace it with open arms.

Commit to a larger institution

If the notion of commitment still feels a little distant, consider committing to something bigger than you. The accountability of committing to a larger institution brings a different set of obligations and responsibilities with it. Fear of commitment may be addressed by committing to something larger than oneself in a group, where you can tap into the collective energy and moral support of your fellow members.

Those who are part of a dedicated group work together for the greater good of the group. As an example, if your family's objective is to be healthier and fitter, commit to a goal together so that each member can hold the other accountable.

Remember that at any point in time, the commitment you have towards your goals will depend on four factors. These are *the benefits, the difficulties, the resources, and the choices.* The benefits are suggestive of why we are working towards these goals and what we hope to or know we will achieve from them. The difficulties are the troubles that stand between us and the goal—all the hurdles that seemingly thwart linear progress. The resources are the things we need to complete the goal—be it physical resources like money, a geographic location, or invisible resources like time and effort. Finally, the choices are representative of how many alternatives we have to get to the things we want in life.

Whenever you encounter something that interests you and makes you think of committing, consider all the benefits and the positive aspects of investing yourself completely in it—with the knowledge that once you commit, you must see things through to the end.

The benefits can represent anything—from learning a new skill because it will add more value to your life, and make you feel like you've accomplished something valuable, to bolster your resume. You can also factor in measurable benefits like a salary hike, a promotion, higher marks, or a healthier body weight. Whatever drives you and presents itself as a reason behind working towards the goal will suffice, so take heed of everything positive that presents itself to you. Your commitment will be higher when you perceive important benefits, so the more benefits you have, the more natural your commitment will feel.

You will invariably encounter some obstacles in the path to achieving your goals. Some will be givens—like the time and resources you need to achieve the goal—maybe you need to invest a small amount of money or devote a month to taking a training course. This will involve a cost that you have to take in your stride. Others will come in the form of hurdles you encounter.

Maybe you went in expecting results within a week but it is taking more time.

Know that everybody has different timelines and all the time in the world does not stand to win against the satisfaction you will feel when you finally achieve your goal. Obstacles are part of the journey to success, so be prepared to face them—the obvious ones and the ones that show up unexpectedly—with the knowledge that you have what it takes to emerge successful each time. From a practical perspective, brainstorming helps, so engage in constructive dialogue whenever you can.

Resources are whatever you need to make sure that you are adequately positioned to fulfill a goal. For instance, if you are trying to lose weight by going to the gym, resources include a vehicle (if the gym is far and you cannot walk to it), gym gear, a time slot, and inner resources like resolve and the will to wake up every day and slog it out, even on the days you want to stay in, cover yourself with a blanket, and give up. When you have the resources, commitment mandates that you use them to their fullest extent.

When it comes down to it, as I mentioned before, you always choose whether you will commit or whether you won't. Like much else in life, commitment is dependent upon how much will and motivation you attach to the choice you make to invest in a cause that matters to you, and how much grit and mental strength you display when it comes to fulfilling this cause, regardless of what variables may come in the way.

In the next chapter, we will talk about our next skill—consistency. You cannot be committed without having consistency in your objectives. The ability to succeed in any undertaking hinges on the ability to maintain a level of consistency throughout time. To be consistent, you must commit yourself to achieve your objectives and maintain a laser-like concentration on the steps you need to take to get there. Before we move on to discussing consistency, let us sum up the key points of this chapter.

CHAPTER SUMMARY

- Commitment to anything is the only way to assure that you adhere to and achieve your objectives, no matter how awful the circumstances.
- SMART planning demands that you pick plans that are detailed, measurable, attainable, realistic, and time-bound.
- Once you have a plan, write down all the actions required to execute it. Write it down in a diary or on a notepad or laptop, but make a

copy and post it somewhere you can see it every day, like the fridge or a closet.

- The difficulty is not making a commitment, but keeping it. When you make a commitment and then violate it, you not only lose the trust of others, but also your own.

- Commitment Issues might arise that prevent us from accomplishing our aims. Choose commitment in whatever you do and you will succeed.

- If you have trouble committing to something on an individual basis, find an accountability partner who will keep you motivated to stick to your goals.

- Be open to changes and transformations that may come in the way so that you don't lose the will to act upon your original motivations.

- Revisit your goals from time-to-time so that you can change or reorient them depending on the circumstances.

5

CONSISTENCY

"Being persistent may lead you to the door but consistency is the key which unlocks it."

— KENNY DASINGER

The Merriam-Webster dictionary defines consistency as "a firmness of constitution or character." I will give you a personal example of what consistency means to me. Way back, when I was developing good habits, I began a dream project—in other words, I began the research that you are now reading today. Writing a book is a long, protracted task. There are hours of finding and verifying facts, tying them to emotional situations which are just as real, and then comes the anxiety—will it reach people? Will my readers relate to what I'm trying to say?

The anxiety could become debilitating on occasion—so much so that I had moments when giving up just felt easier than pushing through. But, here we are. The thing that kept me going was my commitment to reaching out, to the notion that even if ten of you were to pick this book up and find that it had left a positive impact on your life—it would be something to be thankful for. That was the commitment. Then came the consistent adherence to it, irrespective of the good days or the bad. It was consistency that ensured I kept my promise to myself, and that this book found its way to your arms and heart. It is one of the most powerful skills you will develop, and something that will help you stick to whatever plans you make without fail—even if circumstances are not always in your favor.

In my experience, success takes time and work—and I speak for any kind of success. To me, even coming back home after a long day at work and enjoying a cup of tea with full contentment is a measure of how successfully I have conducted the events of the day. Consistency helps me ensure that if I say I will do something, I do it. Because of this, I am able to feel relaxed when the day is done—because I have kept my commitments not just to others around me, but to myself.

You may be wondering, consistency sounds good, but how do I know what it really does? Well, let's take a look.

Consistency is a measure of effectiveness in every new task that you take up

Let's say you have found a new hobby, or have begun a new job or a dream project. Obviously, you will understand your effectiveness in terms of how this project works for you. Unless you have attempted this new task over a consistent period and in a steady fashion, you won't know if it is workable. If you take up task A today and then suddenly shift to task B tomorrow, how will you know whether your efforts with task A would have been successful? The route to measuring effectiveness in anything is via consistency.

A great way to ensure consistent commitment to something is to give a project a minimum of six months before you even think of attempting something different. Within these six months, give it your very best. Use all the resources at your disposal, be committed, and perform consistently. Keep notes of your progress and also write down any potential difficulties you find yourself facing. Once six months are over, go through all the details once again, and consider which side of the list looks heavier—the pros or the cons. You will understand whether this plan works on this basis, and if you find something is inconsistent, you can turn your attention to another plan.

Consistency keeps you accountable

Forging ahead, steady as it goes, is being willing to turn up for something again and over again and create outcomes that are comparable over time. That you keep your end of the bargain is a sign of accountability. Do what you say, and you'll be held to account for your actions—in a positive light. When you have a definite goal in mind, it is simpler to keep yourself accountable. You need to be unambiguous about what you're doing after you've established a time and place for yourself to work. In order to succeed, you must have a clear idea of what you want to accomplish and then stick to it consistently.

You'll find it much simpler to attract and retain your ideal clientele if you supplement consistency with accountability. When you are known for your consistent behavior, people look up to you as someone to rely on.

Consistency improves your reputation and gives you relevancy

For natural reasons when you are able to perform consistently, you will be known as someone to fall back on. People will think of you as a solid source of support because you do what you say and you are always keeping your end of the bargain. Building your professional image requires consistency. Maintaining a regular message across all channels will help you to remain on course even in the face of bad evaluations.

Establishing a set of rules to follow is one of the greatest methods to ensure that things happen unambiguously. You identify a set of principles that help you stay true to yourself, and because of this, you remain upfront and transparent—two key traits when it comes to building a solid reputation.

When you think about it, consistency is a key factor for success if you are running or starting a business. Volatility can be a treacherous trait for business owners, especially when you are trying to build your image or to prove the worth of your product to others. If your employees or the world at large see you as someone who keeps changing his mind, you will inevitably run into problems—so always build your rapport around an image of consistent effort and knowledge. This will be key to delivering a proper message to both your employees as well as the world at large.

When it comes to leading an organization, you must be able to deliver a clear and consistent set of messages. If you keep changing the things that you stand for, you will cease to be relevant because your employees will consider you to be someone who is a subject of their whims. It is important to maintain a more standardized image, which becomes possible only when you are consistent.

All the small actions that you perform on a consistent basis will result in favorably big outcomes over time. Doing something, in the long run, is bound to provide far more substantial results than taking something up on a whim and giving up on it as soon as something feels tough or irregular. Being consistent will ensure that you attract more opportunities for prosperity in your life because others will always look up to you as someone to fall back on, and therefore to trust.

You may be wondering—consistency sounds like a wonderful trait, but what if it isn't for me? What if I can't show it simply because I am someone who has always been impulsive? Is it something that can be learned? Well, yes.

SO, HOW DO YOU LEARN CONSISTENCY?

Consistency is not a trait that you are born with. In my own experience, the harder someones' life experiences are, the tougher they become, and they learn that the only way to get through life's tribulations with sheer focus and concentration is via consistency. With this, let's look at different ways via which you can develop more consistency in life.

Set a proper plan

Decide what you mean by "consistency" to begin with. Is it necessary to maintain a regular workout schedule? Do you want to produce better work? Want to improve the quality of your relationships by being more accessible and dependable? Set objectives that are both precise and attainable. If you don't know what you're supposed to be doing, it's difficult to stay on track. When embarking on a new route, begin by setting small, attainable objectives with clearly defined outcomes.

Once you've determined your ultimate objective, break it down into smaller, more manageable tasks. In the case of an approaching test, for example, establish the aim of studying for five hours a day for two months in advance. Be explicit in your objectives when you establish them. Avoid vague statements like "I'll study."

Instead, be specific about the timeframe, subject, start and end dates, and other aspects of your study plan.

Sleep properly

Keep a regular bedtime and wake-up time. When you wake up every morning with a pounding headache because you don't get enough sleep, it's difficult to concentrate on anything. Having a regular sleep pattern makes it easier to plan your day since you know when you'll be up and active. You'll be better able to stick with your objectives if you get enough sleep every night. Your preferred activities like meditation, blogging, or doing a workout may be added to your daily routine around the times you get up and go to sleep.

Build a schedule

Set a timetable for your activities. The use of a planner, organizer, calendar or timetable will help you keep track of your commitments. To ensure that you complete all of your tasks on time, you should keep a timetable. You'll be able to see clearly what obligations you can and cannot fulfill. Make use of a wall calendar or a paper organizer. Alternatively, you may use a calendar tool like Google Calendar on your phone.

Set realistic time limits for all of your tasks. The best way to know how much time you'll need to accomplish a job is to allow yourself a buffer, or in other words, to set a larger time frame than you may actually need.

To achieve a bigger objective, such as reducing weight or studying for a year-end test, break it down into smaller, more manageable activities. Consider, for example, setting a daily reminder to do 20 minutes of exercise and making daily food plans in advance.

Ensure that you also get room to breathe between your schedules. Set a few hours or a day in the week where you are just relaxing and doing the things you enjoy. This will rejuvenate you and help you return to your tasks with renewed vigor and energy.

Have consistent routines for when you wake up and go to bed

Setting a consistent morning routine enables you to start your day off on the right foot. You begin with the comfort of knowing that you aren't going to be lurched into anything that you aren't accustomed to and that your morning is a sum of routines that has become comfortable and doable.

Being consistent in your morning routines can benefit how you spend the rest of your day because once you get into the mode of being productive, it will likely spill into everything else you do during the course of the day as well. If you have a bad day where you find that nothing is working the way you want it to, morning routines ensure a predictable pattern to return to the next day. Plus, they can also set the clock right for when it is time to go to sleep because you develop a consistent approach to going about the different aspects of your day.

Similarly, night routines ensure that you get a good night's sleep because you know that the moment you are done with the activities that make up this routine, it is time for bed. Being assured of this pattern means that you don't give in to vices like nighttime snacking or sneaking in two hours of Netflix that can extend to early morning, making you feel blurry and groggy.

The more consistently you go to bed, the more centered you will be when you wake up. It's difficult to focus on doing boring tasks when you've been up till four watching a documentary or playing video games, right? You tend to put everything off for the next day. Developing a consistent night schedule ensures that you don't procrastinate when the morning comes and that you are poised to treat each day with focus and good energy.

Make realistic promises

We all love to say that we will help others. But, when you are practicing consistency, remember that you are only making the commitments that you can keep. If you make too many of them, the overwhelming feeling that follows may become a legitimate ground to give up on all of them—so if a request for help comes along and you feel that you simply cannot fit it into your schedule, learn to say "no."

For instance, if your spouse requests you to help with the household chores one day, make sure that you have the time and bandwidth after your work, and that you act upon the commitment that you make to them. Ensure that you decide which half you will tackle, and when the time comes, don't flake out on the promise that you have made. If someone needs your help on a specific day, and you find that your schedule is all booked up in the morning, negotiate if helping the person concerned is important to you. Let them know that you will be available later in the day and show up and keep the promise that you made.

Also, be true to the promises you make to yourself. Don't set unrealistic and wishful goals that you intrinsically know you will walk out on. Instead, set small, achievable tasks which will make you proud when you accomplish them. The key is to do a little bit of something at a time and to do it with absolute concentration.

Focus on habit formation rather than doing things on impulse

You want to develop a routine that encapsulates a consistent flow of habits from one to the next. To do this, start small. For instance, if you are making the habit of working out, don't begin with an hour a day. Instead, start off with 15 minutes and then build on this gradually. Starting small will help you stick to the workout without getting demotivated or also acquiring mind-numbing body aches. As you get more and more proficient, you can focus on increasing the time allotted by ten minutes every ten days.

Try habit stacking or habit chaining to get around your routines. This is the process of clubbing small activities into a routine where you link to a habit that has already been set within your day. You use the things you already do to remember to do something else that you would like to do. For example, if you go to bed at night, this is habit A. You use habit A as the ground to stack another habit—like reading ten pages of a novel. This makes it possible for a routine to become more memorable—and you kind of develop it as a comfort activity. So, reading a book before going to sleep just becomes something that you do.

Finally, remember to celebrate the small wins

Every time you achieve something, remember that it is a feat to be celebrated. The smallest of goals deserve recognition because the latter serves as an indispensable means to keep you motivated in the long run. So, if you have completed your daily chores within the set frame of 6pm, take the evening off to see a film or to enjoy a special dinner.

Read a book that makes you happy or call a close friend. If you are training for a marathon and you have been showing steady progress at the gym, reward yourself by actually signing up for the marathon so that you can measure your progress. If you have finished writing the first fifty pages of your book, celebrate by taking your close friends or loved ones out to an intimate dinner. Do things that will also give you absolute and complete joy.

Consistency is one of the most important determinants of mental toughness

We know by now that mental toughness means getting back in the ring, no matter what difficulties we encounter along the way. It requires a great deal of consistent commitment to ensure that no matter what, we always find the strength to push through and stick to the plans that we make. Consistency becomes important because mental toughness mandates focus on developing a skill and performing that when the time comes. This means that we need to devote consistent focus when we are in the process of learning something.

To illustrate, there was a time when I planned to run a 10k marathon. I was very unfit then, getting out of the string of bad habits that had consumed my life, and also getting the hang of how dreary life could get when you didn't have things to kick back to. I was, however, finding new ways to stay happy and focused, and looking after my health was one of them. Practicing running for the marathon changed a lot of things for me. I had not factored in how much time or work this would take, for I just presumed that I'd be running. The dedication, the grit, and the sheer patience that the whole task involved were completely new for me, and I found myself really struggling.

Plus, there were so many other variables—I had to cater to a completely new diet, schedule my work around the time I invested in preparing for the marathon, and most of all, I had to develop discipline—something that was entirely missing from my life. The more time I invested in consistent preparation, the more I learned about how strong I was mentally.

I found that I had the strength to get over the dark days, to stick to my routines, and to push through even when my legs ached and my heart was heavy. Dear reader, the day I completed that 10k run was one of the proudest days of my life. It taught me so much about myself, most of all about how mentally capable and tough I was. The only way to do it was through the consistent devotion I gave during the preparation stage. If I can do it, so can you.

I guess what I am trying to say is that in life, there will always be difficulties. The trick is to remain consistent, no matter what.

How do you remain consistent?

Consistency is the most difficult thing to achieve in life, but it is also the most important. You must be consistent to learn and perfect an ability, a practice, or a new way of life. So, how can we keep ourselves from straying from the path of consistency?

A great way to begin is to make the conscious choice to be committed to *every task that you take up.* Every morning when you wake up, take the time to repeat this affirmation to yourself: *"I choose to be committed to be consistent in each task that I will undertake today, be it cooking my meals, going to work, taking a walk, or going to sleep at the right time."* When you make this affirmation, you authorize your subconscious to act on the way you desire to live your life in the immediate present tense, rather than pushing it to some unforeseeable future circumstance. Afterall, consistent actions are mandated on being able to think consistently, especially thoughts that enforce that you are and that you will remain consistent.

Act in the present moment rather than always pushing things for the future. Internalize the concept that the only time given to you is the time that you have right now. Truthfully, the whole concept of the future is something that is uncertain, and it is a mere product of your mind. You are not existing in the phase of "tomorrow or next week or next month or next year." You are existing in the phase that is "today—the here and now." The greatest gift you can give yourself is to be in the present moment and to treat your existing state of being with as much discipline and consistency as you can. Choose to be consistent within this very moment. Internalize the need to be attentive in your present state of existence and to consistently perform within the parameters of what is happening right now.

Have a clear sense of your objectives. If you don't want it, you can't have it—it's as simple as that. Keep a plan that has been successful for you in the past and that you know will help you accomplish your objectives today.

When you have a plan in place, you don't need to waste excess time in thinking about what to do—so you are essentially prepared to act in the moment. Plans are key to success, from the smallest ones to the bigger ones.

For instance, you can plan to study for four hours each day, or you can plan your meals a week ahead, or you can set aside a consistent time for working out every day. You must have a strategy in place so that you determine where to put your time, effort, and attention. Whatever you decide to do, be sure it's in keeping with your core principles and what you really want. To succeed in your strategy, you must have a strong emotional connection with it and be able to stay dedicated to it.

Don't give in to the flow of negative emotions. I know they can be very daunting, but they are only transient. They shouldn't mandate what you achieve in life. Any bad feelings or thoughts that can interfere with your ability to remain consistent are just momentary.

It's a tremendous sensation right now, but it may be completely different in a month, twenty minutes, or even tomorrow. Do not succumb to the temptation to succumb to the illusions of pressure, fear, anxiety, or uncertainty. Execute. Exercise, eat a healthy meal, or get back to that project. Keep reminding yourself of how good you'll feel after you've finished your exercise or when you've overcome the obstacle. It will all be worth it in the end.

Finally, seek to always act properly in each little task you do. Higher productivity, less stress and greater happiness may be achieved by emphasizing single-tasking. If you concentrate on one goal at a time, you can accomplish practically everything in life. When a person just works on one thing at a time, they get better outcomes faster. Because multitasking is more exhausting, we end up with unproductivity in the long run. Small things like daily chores feel exhausting and overwhelming, causing you to fall behind on your daily routine and worrying you out.

However, you will experience less stress and even begin to love your job when you concentrate all of your attention on a single activity. How much we achieve is more important than how much time we spend working on it. Productivity isn't about how many tasks we complete, but how much we gain within the time frame of our work. *If we do ten tasks and make a mess out of all of them, we've achieved nothing. If we do one with consistent focus and attention and obtain a successful impact, we have achieved everything.*

Even when we know that consistency is a wonderful thing, it can still feel like it's always slipping out of our hands. It often feels difficult, especially if we are more fixated on the outcome rather than the process or the work that we have to put in. We get too involved with the notion of what will be the result rather than the input that the journey is supposed to focus on. As a result, we end up quitting during the struggle far before we can reap the rewards of staying on track.

BARRIERS TO CONSISTENCY

When you think about it, consistency is a far more important train than doing something with intensity. Intensity is fine, but when you develop it only a few days ahead of a big event, it is bound to leave you exhausted. For instance, if you decide that you will put in twelve hours of study time three days before an examination, you will be far more exhausted than if you study consistently for four hours every day a month ahead of your examinations. Consistency can often feel like a difficult skill to master—and that is okay. Here are five reasons why it is elusive.

1. Some of us invest far too much on motivation

When we rely too much on those "sudden bursts of motivation," we feel that we absolutely cannot do anything until we feel "motivated" enough to do so. So we cycle between periods of extreme efficiency and then periods of doing absolutely nothing. It is important to seek a balance between productivity, motivation, and consistency. The truth is that there will always be days when motivation doesn't feel as strong, where we feel that it is easier to give up than to stick to something. To be consistent means that we get over these periods and stick to our routines simply because we know that the end result of sticking to them is much more favorable than giving up on them.

2. A lot of us procrastinate

We believe in a stream of endless tomorrows, and the moment a tomorrow rolls in, we get tired and frustrated and say, "let me just begin on Monday," "let me start on the New Year's Day," "let me begin on the first of the month,"—and this feeling invariably slows down progress and makes it impossible to develop consistent focus and energy into doing something. Procrastination is kind of synonymous with giving up before you have even begun—and you cannot be consistent if you start off with zero energy or inclination to do something.

3. You may be distracted easily

This becomes a problem especially if you are supposed to focus on one thing but other distractions keep coming in the way and thwarting the amount of time and priority you are supposed to be giving to the one main task. Bad vices make it impossible to focus on something—we tend to deflect by taking breaks to eat junk food, watch a show, or do a hundred other things than the task we should be doing. Another issue with distractions comes through when you develop a plethora of competing priorities which can hamper the attention and work you are supposed to invest into each. It is always better to do one thing at a time and to do it well.

4. The presence and pervasiveness of negative emotions can make it very difficult to stick to your plans.

If you wake up overcome with sadness, lethargy, anxiety or frustration, it can become overwhelming to stick to something when you just want to give in to the tirade of your emotions and go back to sleep.

5. Some things may be outside your realm of control

This is perhaps the hardest determinant of them all, because how can you stay consistent when something unexpected like a sickness, having to stall due to an emergency, or any contingency happens? The important thing in these situations is to return to a consistent pattern of action when things normalize and to ensure that when you feel fit enough to return to the task you had set for yourself, you do so with consistent focus.

The most important determinant of consistency in the wake of all these barriers is to ensure that you stay the course irrespective of the struggles you encounter. If you are facing dire difficulties one day and you need to pause, do it. But don't let the impact of not doing something one day because you needed a necessary break extend to the next day and the one after that.

As soon as you can, return to your task with as much discipline and attention as you can, and ensure that you remain consistent in terms of the work you put into it every day. This is the only way by which you can break the barriers of consistency. In other words, don't let one bad day get in the way of all the work you have already done. Stick to the course, do your best, and live every moment with the intent and purpose to do as good of a job as you can.

Before moving to the next chapter, let's talk about some ways in which you can improve consistency. In successful people, it is the tasks that they do every day, in fixed patterns, that allow for the outcomes that they desire.

HABITS TO IMPROVE CONSISTENCY

There is a law called Wolff's Law which mentions that your body will conform and adapt to the directions and potencies that it is continually subjected to. The word to focus on here is "continually." Doing something once —like working out once in a blue moon and expecting to lose five pounds or develop increased fitness the very next day is unrealistic. The commitments that last are the ones that you stick to continually—so it is only when you consistently commit to becoming healthy over time that you notice the progress you so desire. There are some things you can do to increase your consistency and improve your chances of success. Let's take a look at them.

- Set realistic goals that you will be able to achieve. Follow SMART principles to set your goals, making ones that are Specific, Measurable, Achievable, Realistic, and Time-bound. Setting SMART Goals enables you to concentrate your time and energy in a manner that enhances your chances of success while also helping you to concentrate your thinking and actions.
- Use reminders for new habits. When you are attempting to alter your schedule, it isn't

uncommon to underestimate new obligations and phone calls. Put reminders in places where you can see them throughout the day, so you don't forget about them. Reminders will help you to ensure that you stick to your new schedule and to perform allotted activities consistently.

- Making a mistake is perfectly acceptable. It doesn't imply that you've ruined your consistency even if you violate a vow, skip a target, or cancel on someone. The truth of the matter is that obstacles posed by outside forces do exist. We must prepare for these external circumstances and strive to avoid them from derailing our progress. So, if you do end up skipping on something because of a contingency, tell the people you committed to that there were forces outside your control and promise them delivery on the earliest possible date—and ensure that you remain committed to delivery within this date.

- Keep a list of your objectives. Look at them from time to time whenever you need motivation. Even if you don't feel like it, this might act as an incentive to get everything done throughout the day. To boost your self-discipline, it is important to follow these basic measures. The goals can be the simplest of things like cooking your lunch or going for a walk to something more ambitious like meeting a work deadline.

- Finally, make time for yourself if you are new to the concepts of consistency and routine formation. Realistically, it takes time to get things done. It's not easy to alter your way of thinking, and you may not notice improvements for some time. It might be challenging to change your whole way of life at once with a slew of new habits. Allow yourself plenty of time to ensure the best outcomes best for you and go one new habit at a time.

In the next chapter, we will talk about mindfulness. Practicing mindfulness may enable us to better control our emotions, and alleviate stress, tension, and unhappiness. Focusing our attention and keeping an open mind while observing our thoughts and sensations are all possible through a lifestyle that incorporates mindfulness—and what better way to develop mental toughness than by establishing a deeper connection with yourself? Before we begin, let's take a minute to wrap up the key points we covered in this chapter.

CHAPTER SUMMARY

- Consistency is the key to long-lasting success.
- Giving a project at least six months before considering switching it up is a wonderful method to assure consistency.
- Consistency will guarantee that you attract more prospects for success since people will always look up to you as a reliable source of information.
- You may create a pattern that will help you generate greater consistency in your everyday life by sleeping well and getting up on time.
- Consistency is key for mental toughness since the latter requires focusing on learning and executing a skill in the wake of any difficulties.

6

MINDFULNESS

"Mindfulness is a way of befriending ourselves and our experience."

— JON KABAT ZINN

The concept of mindfulness seems simple enough. You just have to be present in the things that you do. But, really think. When was the last time that you enjoyed a meal completely and without any distractions? When did you read the last book without bothering about little things happening around you? When was the last time you were truly, completely, and wholly invested in the activity you were engaged in?

It's not quite that simple. Mindfulness suggests that your mind is completely attuned to its present state of existence—to the things that you are doing, the space that you are moving through, and the emotions that you are feeling. At a cursory glance, this may seem unimportant, but when you think of how easily our mind veers off-course, how frequently we lose focus and then give up on what we are doing completely, you can begin to make sense of the need to be mindful.

Mindfulness is a way to reestablish your relationship with your body so that you become more than the obsessive thoughts which consume your focus, derail your progress, and weaken your resolve. In other words, you cannot develop mental toughness if you are not present in the moment, and you cannot be present in the moment without mindfulness.

So many of us live on autopilot mode, going through our day-to-day activities with perfunctory carelessness. We forget to stop and revel in everything, so much so that we need relaxation even when we are relaxing— like needing to watch a film or a series when we are enjoying a good meal. We are hardly aware of the things we are experiencing, or the things are missing out on—smells, sights, beautiful connections, and little joys. Our minds are either caught up or we are always thinking of the nonexistent future or the out-of-our-control past.

Mindfulness steps in as the intrinsic habit to be fully aware and present in the moment, with complete recognition of where we are and what we are doing, and the strength to not be overwhelmed by either of these circumstances. This is important, for sometimes when we do live in the present, we can often become instantly reactive and make a mess out of everything by thinking that nothing in the present moment is working out the way we want it to.

Mindfulness doesn't make these judgments, rather, it allows you to live in the present and to *enjoy it.* We may gain considerable mastery over our responses and habitual thoughts by training the mind. The pause allows us to reassess the issue, get a better understanding of it, and react more effectively. When you begin to internalize mindfulness, you gain a deeper understanding of your present, and why it is *exactly the state of being that you need to exist in.*

Let's look at this from the perspective of a definition by the American Psychological Association. They note that mindfulness is an *"awareness of experience with no judgment. It is a state and not a trait. It may be promoted by certain activities or practices, like meditation, but it isn't equivalent to or synonymous with them."*

So, mindfulness is a *state.* This necessarily means that *you can learn it, and it can be inculcated through meticulous practice.* People are not naturally born mindful—it is a practice that involves becoming more aware and honing the impartiality of the self and others around the self as a result of this awareness. In the contemporary context, where the judgment of others has become so grueling and forthcoming, mindfulness can give you immense peace and contentment.

The EOC Institute identifies three types of people concerning levels of mental toughness. These types are the marshmallow, the jelly bean, and finally, the rock (*The Ultimate Guide To Grit, Mental Toughness, & Meditation,* 2022).

The marshmallow, as the name suggests, is squidgy and soft, and can melt or burn with the slightest exposure to any heat or pressure. Jelly beans can withstand some, but not a lot of stress. In time, their hard exteriors fade away and they succumb to the vagaries of the world. This leaves the only people who are capable of surviving a storm, irrespective of the circumstances. *The rocks.*

Does mindfulness contribute to your becoming a marshmallow or a rock? As evidence suggests, it does. Let's take a look.

MINDFULNESS LEADS TO MENTAL TOUGHNESS

Mental toughness presents the ability to overcome situations of strength, recover, grow from the pain that the stresses often leave behind, and adapt. In short, it helps people to find ways out of intensely challenging situations and is necessary for any form of true growth.

The thing that you have to understand is that mental toughness isn't just one isolated thing. You can't just get it from training your mind or body in isolation. Optimal toughness results when your entire body is in a harmonious equation with all its component parts. We know that the way to strengthen physical fitness is by going to gyms or working out at home and eating healthy food.

The way to mental fitness is by being mindful. Mindfulness practices like meditation have the power to change the structural and functional constitution of your cognitive capacities. Just as the act of building muscles is the way to prevent any physical injuries and to build physical strength, mindfulness contributes to *mind fitness,* which results in grit and mental toughness. When you develop mindfulness, your brain becomes better equipped to handle and recover from psychological stresses.

About four decades back, Dr. Herbert Benson gave meaning to the term *"relaxation response."* He used it to refer to the creation of deep physical and mental quietude in your body—which acts as the polar opposite of how you feel when your body goes through a stress response. His research provided us with the knowledge that mindfulness practices like prayer, meditation, and yoga can elicit this response, and in turn, contribute to overall well-being.

Benson's study provided the impetus for a 2013 research related to the impact of the relaxation response on gene expression (Bhasin, 2013). The researchers were intent on finding whether a singular session of RR-inducing practices would immediately impact upon gene expression. Cellular differentiation, proliferation, patterning, biologic plasticity, and adaptation are all dependent on gene expression regulation. This suggests that gene control may act as a basis for evolutionary change. In simple words, we need gene expression to evolve into our best selves.

The research team also worked to find out whether there were any differences in terms of long-term or short-term practice of relaxation techniques. They enlisted 26 participants with zero RR experience. The participants were assessed at the beginning of and at the end of the training program. The results were compared to a control group of participants who regularly practiced some form of relaxation like yoga, meditation, or repetitive incantations.

It was found that RR had induced beneficial gene expression in the participants. Inflammatory responses like stress and cancer were suppressed, while energy metabolism was enhanced. The long-term practitioners enjoyed even more benefits, but the overall results showed that everyone practicing RR, new or old, benefited in terms of gene development.

Another study involving 48 marines found that, compared to soldiers who lacked mindfulness training, those who did reported more positive moods and felt better equipped to do their jobs (Pappas, 2010).

So, you tell me. Today, if you knew that the processes in your body are providing an automatic immunity against stress and dangerous diseases like cancer, would you not feel happier? And when you are more positive and uplifted, is it not easier to feel an overall sense of mental and physical strength?

It's kind of like going to the gym or working out. Some days, you focus on the shoulders. Some days you concentrate on working out your legs (Mindfulness and Mental Toughness, 2022). You don't just go to the gym and say that you are only going to lose belly fat. To lose fat from your belly, you need to work your entire system.

Mental toughness is no different—the important thing is to be in a constant state of training and practice to be the best that you can be. This involves doing everything in an easy and calm mind. The more volatile you are, the bigger the messes you will make.

Summing up, here are some ways in which mindfulness can help increase your mental toughness.

Firstly, your brain gets more processing time. It is possible to shift from high-frequency brain waves, which are associated with mental agitation, to lower-frequency brain waves via mindfulness activities like meditation. There is greater space between ideas when your brain operates more slowly. With more time on your hands, you'll be able to make better decisions about which ideas to spend your time on.

When you get apprehensive, you begin to feel terrified and threatened because of the way the neural centers in the brain process different kinds of information. Mindfulness decreases the potency of these connections. As these ties are severed, your capacity to cope with worry improves. You get the bandwidth to react more logically to feelings such as worry or dread more easily.

Mindfulness helps you to be present and productive within the area that you are currently in. It removes all possible focus that you may be giving to white noise and unnecessary distractions. It draws your attention to the important things at hand. Mindfulness improves memory powers so that you don't have as much difficulty in recalling different information. You are therefore able to have more meaningful conversations, make intentional choices, and forgo any distractions.

Developing a greater capacity for mindfulness might help you cultivate a more positive outlook on life. When you are attentive, you can enjoy life's little joys more thoroughly, become more interested in your work, and have a stronger ability to cope with difficult situations.

Most mindfulness practitioners feel that they have fewer anxieties about the things out of their immediate control—like future worries or past regrets, and can create deep friendships and a profound sense of identity.

A lot can happen when you have established a meaningful relationship with yourself. The most profound of this is the birth of mental toughness and the confidence that you can weather all challenges, under all circumstances.

Now that we know what mindfulness is, and why it is so important, we come to the next focus point—*if it can be built, how do we do it?*

HOW TO PRACTICE MINDFULNESS?

Well, you don't have to do anything too extravagant. Our daily lives offer us ample opportunities to sneak in a few minutes where we can just be our most mindful selves. All we have to do is consciously embrace these opportunities.

Think about this for a second. How often have you bolted out of your house after waking up too late, because you also went to sleep at an ungodly hour? Did you spare so much as a cursory thought to the things you would like to achieve during the course of the day?

If you are anything like what I once was, you would have done both these things. Then, as the day progressed, the tiniest of things would leave me impatient, angry, or frustrated, both with myself and the world around me. Even if I woke up intending to do good, the sheer scattered nature of approaching everything would be enough to undo me. Before I knew it, the day was controlling me instead of being the other way round.

Too much time spent preparing, addressing problems, wondering, or ruminating on the bad or irrational aspects of life is tiring. Stress, worry, and sadness are all things that may be exacerbated by it. Mindfulness exercises may help you refocus your attention on the present moment instead of dwelling on the problems of the past or worrying about the future.

Anywhere and at any moment, simple mindfulness activities may be undertaken so long as you possess the intention of truly practicing them. Taking in the sights and sounds of nature, for example, is a great way to focus on the moment and be mindful.

A peaceful environment with no distractions or interruptions is required for more systematic mindfulness activities like body scan meditation or seated meditation. You may choose to begin your day with this form of workout in the early morning.

For the first six months, try to meditate every day. It's possible that practicing mindfulness may become second nature to you over time. As a commitment to re-establishing and strengthening your relationship with yourself, think of it as something that you are gifting to yourself.

Let us now take a look at how you can make mindfulness a part of your daily routine.

WAKE UP MINDFULLY

Always wake up with good intentions. When we speak of intention, we refer to the deep-seated motivation that compels us to do the things we do or say what we say. When we act impulsively, we give in to the subconscious, faster impulses situated in lower brain zones, while ignoring the more stable decision-making abilities situated at higher centers of our brain (such as the prefrontal cortex).

In other words, when you train your mind, you set yourself apart from a significant chunk of humanity—people who let their unconscious mind rule their day, therefore living unmindfully daily. The practice of setting intentions can marry your conscious thought patterns and associate them with reward centers of the lower brain. So, you do something good with the knowledge that you will feel satisfied because of it.

When you wake up, take a relaxed posture and sit quietly on your bed for five minutes. Keep your eyes closed and take three deep breaths. With each breath, connect with how you are feeling within. Keep your spine straight, and your movements soft.

As you breathe in and out, ensure that the air goes in through your nose and out of your mouth. After three breaths, let your breathing fall into its usual pattern. Simply be aware of the motions of your abdomen and chest when you breathe.

Then, ask yourself, *"what intention will I set for today?"* Choose your answer wisely, based on predictors such as what will leave the best impact on you and those who matter to you, what goals align with your immediate priorities, how you can take care of yourself, and how you can forge meaningful connections. Based on what you decide, set a clear intention for the day.

Remember to check in at different points until it is night and time for you to go to bed. Pause at overwhelming junctures, take deep breaths, and remind yourself what your intentions are. With time, you will feel the impact of this consciousness on your relationships, inner moods, and your inner and outer communications.

CONSUME FOOD MINDFULLY

It is so easy for us to become distracted when we eat. We wolf down our food without pausing to truly feel any of the sensations. Sometimes, we resort to watching shows and forget to even focus on what we are eating—it becomes perfunctory beyond measure.

It is simple enough to just go through the motions—you gobble and swallow. But when was the last time you ate with intention? When you do that, you will notice that it is one of the most pleasurable activities you can partake in. Not just that, when you eat mindfully, you also nourish your body.

Take a deep breath before you eat. Don't rush from one task to the next. Pause, slow down and allow for a seamless transition from whatever you were doing to the task of eating. Focus your energies inward and close your eyes. Count to ten, and then focus on the plate of food in front of you.

Look out for how you are physically feeling in the moment—use a scale as a reference point. Between 0 to 10, how would you rate yourself in terms of being physically hungry? Do you notice an empty stomach, shakiness, growling? Or do you feel full? Do this without thinking about when you ate last—just focus on the present.

As a corollary to the last principle, eat when you feel hungry. Be mindful in choosing when, what, and how much you will eat. This will ensure that you are eating to nourish yourself, and not because you are bored or in need of a distraction.

Slow down and take even breaths while eating. Savor every bite. Feel the textures and different tastes envelop your mouth. Every mouthful should be enjoyable, so transition from one bite to the next with mindful ease.

DO A MINDFUL WORKOUT.

Exercising is a must for a healthy body, but it is also necessary for a healthy mind. Whatever physical activity you take up, do so with intention and the desire to do your utmost best in it. Notice the shift in your body from being distracted and busy to being focused and capable.

Establish a clear aim and do your physical activity mindfully. Be aware of how you want to guide the session—each movement, the time you want to give to it, the length of the overall session—in short, every-thing you do should result from purpose, not a whim.

Take five minutes to work out. Do simple moves to heat up your body so that your muscles don't spasm later on. Jogging in place, taking a five-minute brisk walk, doing stationary jumping jacks—all these are great ways to pace yourself. Match your breathing pattern to the flow of your movement. This will establish a systematic rhythm between your brain, heart, and nervous system.

Breathe evenly throughout your workout. Follow a consistent rhythm. Your workout doesn't have to be an hour-long sweat fest. So long as you give fifteen minutes with mindfulness, you'll have done enough. Once you establish a steady breathing pattern, follow this to the end of the workout.

Spend the last ten minutes before you cool down by challenging yourself. Try more repetitions or raise your speed. You can also lift heavier weights or break into a run from a jog—depending on the kind of activity you are doing. Move beyond the discomfort to see whether you feel alive, alert, and conscious of every physical movement.

Take five minutes to cool down. Slow your pace before relaxing on the floor or halting. Stretch your muscles, and take a few relaxing breaths. Notice the sense of accomplishment wash over you and revel in it. *How do you feel? Accomplished? Victorious?* Name this feeling and cherish it. Tell yourself you will seek to feel the same way tomorrow.

In passing, I'd say that we make the exercise of mindfulness to be far more difficult than it truly is. All you have to do is to slow down and take in the surroundings in a world that has become far too busy for its own good. Take time to enjoy and experience the environment and the blessings that your senses have vested unto you.

Live in the moment and find joy in simple things—a pretty sunrise, a hot cup of coffee on a chilly morning, or an hour with a loved one. Love yourself for who you are, and you will find that mindfulness brings you closer to everyone else. Finally, when negative thoughts take over, sit down, take a deep breath and focus on its flow. Then say this,

"I choose to do the best I can. That much is up to me."

In the next chapter, we will talk about the skill of resourcefulness, and how it can get you closer to your objectives. Before that, let us take a minute to sum up the key points we read in this chapter.

CHAPTER SUMMARY

- Mindfulness can be developed with practice.
- Daily activities can incorporate mindfulness.
- When you develop mindfulness, you not only feel relaxed but also enable positive gene expression.
- Mindfulness is important in developing mental toughness.

- Whenever you feel overwhelmed, always pause and take a few deep breaths.
- Ensure that you begin each day with the intention and the will to do well. Tackle things mindfully and you will do well.

7

RESOURCEFULNESS

How do you define resourcefulness? Before we move into this chapter, let me ask you this—what does the concept of resourcefulness imply when you think about it?

If you asked me, resourcefulness represents the ability to make your own decisions and be responsible for your actions. A resourceful person is someone who can come up with different means to handle any situation that comes their way.

Let me share an interesting story with you.

Did you know that Amazon started out as a simple online bookstore? Look at where it is today. It has become a wonderland where everything—food, beauty, health, wellness, gadgets has become available for your interest and consumption.

How did it become a retailer of pretty much everything that the world has to offer in just about a decade from where it began? Well, Amazon's founder Jeff Bezos shared some insights into the growth of Amazon at a summit in Los Angeles in 2017.

He talked about the importance of resourcefulness— over his Ivy League education, as something that had been instrumental to his success (McKissen, 2019). He would go on to say that the whole agenda behind moving things ahead is that while you will run into problems, you need to find ways to tackle them and keep trying.

Every attempt that you make to get back up after you've been knocked into the dust is an example of resource- fulness—of being self-reliant. You are looking at a way of life that isn't restricted to the claustrophobic comfort of four walls. You're becoming open to learning, under- standing, and accepting that things may not always go your way. All while also fortifying the faith that you will find ways to buckle up and try once again.

Let's look at another example of what resourcefulness can do for you. Chesky's *air mattress with a bed and breakfast* company began as a personal whim, but he developed it into a hospitality industry behemoth. Today, there are 6 million listings on Airbnb, and two million people use the service every night. Travelers can now customize their vacations with the debut of the company's new Trips feature.

Why is resourcefulness such an important skill, not just for mental toughness, but also in general?

Firstly, resourcefulness is an essential tool to develop stamina. It enables you to look at your constraints in a new light. You stop considering them from the viewpoint of how troublesome they are. Instead, you begin to appreciate their value in helping you learn more about yourself and how much you are capable of. The deeper you delve into this self-knowledge, the more innovative solutions you are capable of finding.

Mental toughness is all about withstanding challenging situations. When you are resourceful, you understand that you will find ways to tackle each troublesome circumstance and make something good out of it. The concept of a challenge will not make you afraid or intimidate you—rather, it will inspire you.

Resourcefulness will give you the tools to tackle difficult issues with simple solutions. It will teach you to approach the world in a new light. You will be able to generate maximum value right now, instead of constantly worrying about the future or feeling sorry for the past.

When faced with unexpected and unforeseeable challenges, it is important to be resourceful. It's not a feature you're born with, but rather an expression of other qualities that may be gained through time, such as wisdom, passion, and an innovative attitude.

Most of all, resourcefulness is closely linked to mental toughness since it pushes people to actively seek out possibilities for personal progress because they have a high degree of confidence in their talents.

Resilient leaders provide a collaborative environment in which problems are discussed openly and solutions are devised as a group. They are open to new ideas, willing to try new approaches, and able to work well with others. To be a resourceful leader, the first thing that you have to do is appreciate the importance of people as a resource. How do you do that?

VALUING PEOPLE AS A RESOURCE

In terms of securing high employee engagement and retention rates, two important questions can be found across industries. Firstly, are your employees feeling valued within the organization? And secondly, does the workforce have faith in the overall vision of the organization and the capabilities of the leader?

It may surprise you, but these two questions can have a 76% connection with how employees perform within an organization, and whether they stay in one place for an extended time or keep looking for better opportunities. If your company has a poor retention rate, it is likely related to problems in either one or both of these areas.

Employee benefits have a 49 percent link and fair pay has a 60 percent correlation to increased levels of employee engagement (*How to Value Your Employees as the Most Important Resource, 2022*). Also, in companies where employees feel valued and have faith in the leadership, there is greater productivity, more client satisfaction, and lower voluntary turnover rates.

In an enterprise, it's the employees who get things done. How the company operates and how their own team functions best is something they have a deep understanding of. To accomplish their tasks in a timely and efficient manner, they know the procedures and technologies to use.

Additionally, they often interact with consumers, which means they have a better understanding of what the client is considering and what they need. More than anything else, this is priceless. People are a company's most precious resource because they can foresee issues, provide suggestions for improvements, and deliver on their promises to customers.

If you are looking for ways to improve employee retention and induce higher engagement rates in your workforce, you must be committed to valuing the people who work in your organization. Remember that they are spending eight to ten hours five days a week, sometimes six, in your office. That's a significant chunk of their whole lives. If they do not feel appreciated, it is unlikely that they will look for reasons to stay.

To generate value among your employees, you can follow the directions in the table below.

Foundation	Associate	Chartered Member	Chartered Fellow
This level requires you to:	This level requires you to:	This level requires you to:	This level requires you to:
Develop an understanding of your work's purpose.	Build team spirit and a sense of purpose among colleagues.	Motivate and inspire others by effectively articulating the significance and goal of the work they are doing.	Inspire others with a compelling vision for the future of the workplace that reflects the larger purpose and direction of the job.
Treat others with empathy.	Be impartial in your valuation of others.	Exhibit a compassionate and just approach.	Become the embodiment of what people will identify as a "fair and just" leader.
Encourage people to grow and achieve their full potential.	Providing opportunities for people to learn and grow to perform at their peak levels in work	Empower executives and leaders to help their subordinates perform at their highest level in the office.	As a means of building operational effectiveness and benefiting society, promote and support professional life learning
Offer constructive advice to your colleagues and managers.	Do your best to help and guide people in the industry.	Educate, counsel, and empower your company's employees in the area of human resources management.	In the workplace, cultivate a climate of responsibility for effective personnel management.
Seek the advice of a diverse group of individuals and pay close attention to their comments.	Make it possible for individuals to have a say in the design and implementation of products and services that affect them	Assist workers in making choices that affect their lives by allowing them to participate in the decision-making process.	Make an effort to cultivate a corporate culture that empowers employees and places them at the heart of all they do.
Take into account the needs of others	When designing and delivering your job, think about the well-being of others.	Foster the economic and humanitarian implications of well-being as well as the need for mutual accountability among all employees.	Assist in the development and maintenance of an environment that promotes health and well-being.

CHARTERED MEMBER: CHARTERED FELLOW

It is always beneficial to give your employees the respect that they deserve. By doing this, not only are you enabling a culture based on mutual understanding and cooperativeness, but you are also encouraging your employees to put their best foot forward at all times. It is a mark of a truly mentally tough leader to look after the health and wellbeing of the people in their organization. The more you do this, the higher your overall productivity will be.

Now that we know how resourcefulness can be brought about in your office, our next agenda is—how do you go about bringing it into your personal life?

HOW TO BUILD RESOURCEFULNESS

We already know that being resourceful means that you can elicit the information, products, services, and resources that you want. You may think that this is a talent to be born with—but believe me, nobody has solutions handed to them on a silver platter. Something or the other will always fall short of our expectations—be it in relationships, professions, or just daily life.

Whenever you feel a pinch incoming, think of creative ways in which you can counter the situation. Resourcefulness will help you solve the problems that come your way—so that you eventually learn to produce more with less. It is not a talent, it is a skill that is honed.

First, be open to any chances you get to solve problems

Be creative in your ideas and solutions. Always be proud of your accomplishments. Making sure that any mistakes are negligible in comparison to the reward is the key.

If you go over the line, be prepared to accept responsibility, make amends, or explain yourself. Rules are in place for a good purpose, but they may also stifle growth when they're applied incorrectly. Don't simply go along with the way things are just because it is the "norm", rather, try to think of what will be the best for you in any given situation.

Always think of how you can include improvisations

Try to get out of the box of conventional thinking. Sometimes, just devising a temporary solution can be very helpful—and leave you with more room and creative space to think of a long-term solution. So, if you are faced with an immediate issue, think of what you would do so that you can just get by in the moment, and then consider what a long-term solution may require from you.

Be open to experiments and trial and error. Even if you stumble, you will understand what works, and what doesn't. Be adaptive—just because one solution has worked for a hundred others, it doesn't mean that it will work the same way for you. Draw inspiration from others but don't become reliant on their opinions to do what is right or wrong. Instead, use your willpower to find out what you can do in any challenging situation.

Be confident in your creativity

The more you tap into your creative energies, the more you'll be able to find different solutions to problems. To build your creative energies, focus on a topic that will allow you to express yourself unconventionally. Anything that will get your brain to think works—even if it is just learning the tune to a new song or picking up a paintbrush or recording a vlog. As you get adept at doing things in your personal life with creative energy, transition to implementing creative choices in your workplace as well.

Always remember that creativity is something you tap into. Streamline your life for optimum creativity by removing obstacles, generating a feeling of order, and attaining clarity of mind via contemplation. This may make a great impact.

Use challenging situations to your advantage

Remember that every situation presents some positives and negatives. Instead of focusing on the inherently good or bad aspects of it, consider what outcomes you can generate from the situation right now—and how they may help you in the future.

If you're scared, turn that apprehension into fuel for your purpose.

You'll be motivated to find a way out of a difficult position. Make the most of it by brainstorming a solution and putting it into action. When used properly, emotions may serve as powerful motivators for achieving higher levels of quality and efficiency.

Make a conscious effort to build new skills

Actively seek ways to utilize your creativity and perspective. It helps to keep an open mind and to always be in the pursuit of new skills, because the more you learn, the more you will be able to understand.

You will develop a deep understanding of who you are and where your intrinsic capabilities lie. You can get out of a funk by learning a new skill. If you don't acquire new abilities, you run the risk of becoming cognitively and physiologically stale as a result of continuously falling into the same pitfalls of old habits and faulty mindsets.

In passing, I'd say that just have an intrinsic awareness of where your core skills lie. If you find that you aren't able to handle something on your own, never be afraid of asking for help. Sometimes, the best solutions come out of teamwork and collaboration—so be open to reaching out.

THE ART OF IMPROVISATION

When I think of what resourcefulness needs from us, I keep coming across one concept that you may or may not be familiar with—improvisation. Have you ever been part of a situation where things just fell a little off-track, and you had to do something outside your routine plan to ensure that the flow was maintained? I had to improvise all through my youth and adult life—I just wasn't aware that I was doing it. The more I studied about habits and how to build resourcefulness, the more I realized how adept we are at changing and adapting to circumstances, only if we are willing to try.

Let me share an example. I was part of a big team meeting for a product launch. We spent months developing the intel on this product, and I made a truckload of important charts to share this intel with the board members in my office. Then, when the day came, I left for the office, and on reaching the meeting—found that I had forgotten to bring the charts.

I could have panicked, but I chose to think outside the box. I made the entire session interactive. I used the board to draw some figures and charts on the spot. I had extensive knowledge of the topic of discussion. While I shared this knowledge, I also involved the board members and elicited their opinions and feedback. Together, we built something ten times better than what I would have made if I'd have worked alone. What was instrumental here was my willingness to experiment, think out of the box, and come up with new solutions on the spot.

This, in a nutshell, is improvisation.

Improvisation involves acting and reacting based on one's immediate surroundings and in response to the occurrence of events within these immediate surroundings. If done correctly, it can lead to new ways of thinking and acting that can sometimes be even more beneficial than the original ways. The way to do this is via a deep understanding of the topic or skills that one is improvising. So, you can't make up an impromptu music piece if you have no idea about the basic notations. Once you have the basics down, improvisation becomes easy.

Mental toughness requires you to be responsive to sudden changes in your circumstances. With improvisation, you can respond to these changes intuitively, and with new solutions. The two are fundamentally related to one another. Since improvisation helps you to devise new ways of moving forward, it needs a level of grit from your side.

Improvisation is all about acting without a plan to follow, which means you have to make quick judgments about what you're going to say or do next. Due to the lack of time, this exercise improves your ability to make quick decisions. You're compelled to commit to the choices you make and take ownership of the consequences.

If you become anxious and overwhelmed the moment something goes awry, neither will you exhibit mental toughness, nor will you be able to improvise. The act of improvising is an art that requires calm logic and creative spirit, and most of all—the grit to know that you will find a way out of the difficult situation.

So, the next time you come across a difficult situation, here are the things you can do to improvise. These techniques have been shared by American actor Bill Murray—and who knows improvisation better than people who have to do it on screen every day?

- Always listen with intent. To know what you will say next, you need to have an acute understanding of what came before. When engaging in an important conversation, don't turn your attention to anything else. Keep your entire focus on what is being said at the moment.

To be able to respond appropriately in any situation, you must first understand the thoughts and feelings of the other individuals involved. As you listen, put yourself in their shoes to gain a sense of their motives and try to experience what they are going through. By connecting and engaging, you may have access to a wealth of information.

- Say "yes" to situations, and try to relinquish control. This may feel naturally contradictory at times, especially when you are used to naturally being at the helm of affairs. Improvisation means that you are no longer concerned with one strict plan—all you need to do is something that will lead to the desired outcome.

So, whatever plan you take up, simply adjust your expectations as long as it leads to the final goal in sight.

If you are open to accepting all unplanned things that come your way, you embrace the concept of uncertainty and choose to react even if things get difficult. This makes you mentally tough and also earns you the respect of others. It also becomes easy for you to find solutions when you aren't fighting against the change that will inevitably happen.

- Always commit. When improvising, there is no middle ground—you're either in or not. If you choose to pull through, make sure to commit to the choices and actions you make. Keep your mind focused and ready to give quick responses to whatever questions come your way.

The unique thing about improvisation is that there is no "wrong" or "right"—you are just living in and responding to the moment. The only things you are concerned with are action and reaction.

- Finally, practice improvising at home in front of a mirror. This will be helpful for when a real-life situation comes along and tests your improvisation skills. The more comfort you establish with treading into the unknown beforehand, the easier it will be for you to implement it later on.

The worst enemies that can come your way when you are trying to get something done are excuses. Seek to innovate in your daily office life, whenever you can. You may be wondering how innovation can come through in everything that you do—and you'd be surprised. Let's take a look at what you can do to innovate daily.

MAKE THINGS HAPPEN, NO MATTER WHAT

In daily life, particularly in your workplace, you will sometimes find that to make any impact, you need to innovate. The crucial thing here is to make things happen—and innovation is the key to creation. Little things that you do can have a big impact on your ability to innovate. So, as a leader, how can you seek to constantly innovate? Let's take a look.

When conducting meetings, try to stand and talk to others

Standing meetings exudes a different kind of energy—and you'd be surprised at the increase in momentum, action, and enthusiasm among your employees when you do a meeting standing up instead of sitting with your noses buried in paperwork. The act of standing makes it likely that you are inspired to take action. So, your employees will feel encouraged to move quickly and think of solutions.

Seek to be inspired

By enabling us to overcome our everyday experiences and limits, inspiration allows us to open our minds to new possibilities. When we are inspired, we are driven from complacency to possibilities and our perception of our skills is transformed.

Start small

Big, revolutionary, or groundbreaking are all terms we use to describe concepts that we believe should always be in the realm of possibility. But in many cases, it's a series of modest, original actions that may have a big impact.

Small-scale innovation has enormous advantages. In addition to the fact that they can be implemented quickly and with little trouble, they also serve as a stepping stone for greater, more sophisticated innovation initiatives. Consider making a variety of tiny adjustments, such as altering the way you sign off emails, how you begin meetings or the ways in which you appreciate good behavior.

Get a friend

This is a lot like getting an accountability partner—sometimes, the best decisions don't happen singularly, but when you are surrounded by others who will guide and help you in the process. Seek advice from your friend, ask them how they would react to spontaneous situations, and then mold your thoughts and actions.

Finally, take action

Sharing your thoughts and views is necessary, but you must proceed with concrete action. Once you have given a voice to your thoughts, move into building blueprints for action. Once people around you can clearly envision your plans, they will be able to take things seriously and put much more attention to the developmental processes.

Before we move on to the next and final chapter, I will leave an earnest request for you.

DITCH THE EXCUSES.

The next time you find yourself getting bogged down by excuses, try to think of what you could do if there were no "buts" or "ifs."

Give credence to your inner voice. Sometimes, regardless of your hardest efforts and best intentions, something will just not work out. When you find that you cannot overcome an issue, simply accept it and move ahead with the learning that it brings. Life can throw unmanageable situations in our direction at times, and the brave thing to do lies in living despite these situations. If you feel that you can come up with a solution in time, think, devise strategies and be calm—but always be practical and honest with yourself.

Make small, measurable, and observable goals. If you set a lofty goal like "I want to lose thirty pounds in a month," all you will end up attracting is immense hardship, frustration, and a dangerous health issue. Instead, break this goal up into small segments that are more achievable. Aim for four pounds in a month. At the end of the month, when you see that you have fulfilled this goal, you will be the one feeling more empowered and accomplished.

Have faith in your abilities. You can become someone who inspires others. If you don't want to be someone who is watching others change and live their best lives, you can become the person that you wish to be. All humans are naturally capable of evolving and growing —and this includes you. You have to recognize your self-worth to facilitate change, so begin by doing things one step at a time.

Rather than always "wanting" something, act upon achieving it. If you limit yourself to just wanting—you may never get to the action stage. But if you act, you are putting real effort into realizing your vision and the possibility of a future outcome.

And finally, don't judge your progress by the measure of how others are doing in their lives. You don't know which page of their story they're at—and as the saying goes, you can't compare page 3 of your book to page 300 of theirs'. Remember that just because someone else is achieving a goal that is also your dream—*there is absolutely nothing that says that you can't have that goal too.* Ditch the excuses, the blaming, and the guilt, and focus on pure intent and clean actions. In time, the things you desire will come to you.

In the next chapter, we will conclude the discussion of core skills with self-forgiveness. Before that, let's sum up the key points we read in this one.

CHAPTER SUMMARY

- Resourcefulness is important for mental toughness because it teaches you to act with logic in unexpected situations.
- Improvisation is an important skill to learn

how to come up with quick and efficient
solutions on the spot.

- When it comes to both resourcefulness and
improvisation, they are not talents but skills
that can be learned.
- It is important to value an organization's
employees.
- Your excuses may be hindering your progress,
so always act instead of just finding ways to
skirt around the things you need to do.

8

SELF-FORGIVENESS

Sometimes, no matter how hard you try or how good your intentions are, things will fail to go in the ways you expect or want. In these situations, it is important to learn to forgive yourself. Mental toughness mandates that you keep pushing through tough situations—and if you can't forgive yourself for the mistakes you occasionally make, how will you forge ahead?

Let's face it. Slip-ups are expected. We make a minor mistake or an error and that derails our progress. It has happened to all of us. But what is important is picking ourselves up and moving on. You see—*a slip is not necessarily a fall, and neither do you have to make it one.*

Have you ever had the pleasure of watching someone really capable? Like a top athlete, an efficient boss, or anyone with proficiency in what they are doing? These individuals seem to be able to perform with absolute efficiency—at levels that we can only dream of. They seem to be achieving things that always feel out of reach to us.

The thing is, no one who is now at the peak of their game got there without making mistakes. From Michael Jordan and Muhammad Ali to Martha Stewart and Nigella Lawson—each and every successful individual has encountered troubles. Without these troubles, they'd only be stuck within their comfort zones, only doing what was easy and mundane. They chose to make mistakes, forgive themselves, learn and practice and get things right. The only way to do this is by stepping outside the walls of the comfort zone.

The world outside the comfort zone is full of trip-ups and slip-ups. But it is the only way for you to get to the next level. Every time you make a mistake, you gain an opportunity to learn how you can do things better. If you keep repeating the things you are comfortable with —*how will you learn anything new?* Learning goes hand in hand with being able to forgive yourself. When you forgive your errors, you allow yourself to treat your mistakes like tools to learn from.

The next time you slip up, understand that this only means that the learning you have acquired concerning the issue is failing somewhere. The issue isn't with you or your capabilities—it is just that you need to learn to do this thing a little differently. Mistakes are natural—and they will tell you that you are pushing the boundaries of what you already know (and what may have become redundant) to learn new and better things.

When you self-forgive, you choose to acquire deep knowledge on what went wrong. There's evidence that human beings know what they will do with a mistake within 0.25 seconds of making it. They choose two options. Either they ignore the mistake and move on, or they pay attention to where things went wrong and learn how to better their understanding. Ignoring a mistake may seem easier in the short run, but trust me, it will find its way back to you. The wiser thing to do is to take the opportunity to learn from the things that did not work.

To do this, you have to embrace the notion that your mistakes will help you to learn. Enable your brains to comprehend slip-ups as normal, and to look at them with inquisitiveness. Always ask yourself, *"how do I stop this from happening in the future?"*

If you only self-blame and decide you aren't good enough, you may inadvertently lose faith in what you are doing and give up. The issue here is—*how many times will you give up? How many projects will you shun, and how many careers will you change?* At one point, you have to turn your attention inward to find out where your practical knowledge is lacking. The only way to do that is to forgive yourself and embrace your mistakes as opportunities to do things better.

Learning from our errors is essential to progress. While errors are unpleasant, we must teach our minds to examine the mistake, determine what went wrong, and then correct the situation. How do we become better at what we're doing? That's how.

EMPATHIZE WITH YOURSELF

Forgiving yourself and being condescending are not the same thing. So while you should not take your slip-ups personally, treat them with gravity. We make mistakes from the day we are born. We don't learn to walk and talk the moment we shoot out into the world, right? We stumble, we wobble, we give our parents nightmares about if and whether we will finally say the first word.

We make mistakes at school—our whole life, if you look at it, is a measure of the things we did to fix the things that went wrong. So, you already have the tools that are needed to learn from your mistakes.

No matter what happens, it is not a failure to make a mistake. To put it another way, it merely implies you're a fallible being. You can choose to leave everything and bolt whenever an error comes up—therefore learning absolutely nothing.

Alternatively, you might use the error or slip-up as a capacity to experience and improve. You'll be well on your road to achieving your skills if you take this route. For this is how we learn, develop, and become better people.

So, if you make a mistake, don't write yourself off as a failure just because you slipped up. Recognize your vulnerability and use it as a chance to grow.

The first step in this direction is to be kind to your mind.

Think of this. Would you ever call a close friend or someone who matters to you, and tell them depreciative things like—*"you are so useless," "you fail at everything," "nobody loves you,"* or *"you will never succeed."*

No! Then why would you say that to yourself? Aren't you the only person who will accompany you for the entirety of your existence? Then why would you make the journey difficult by berating yourself constantly along the way? You deserve to be kind to yourself, to appreciate who you are, and how far you have come.

Treat yourself like you would treat your friends.

Whenever you find that you are engaging in negative self-talk, get a pen and paper. Draw a table that will have five columns and two rows. Each of the columns will have labels—let me show you.

The Thought	The Emotion	The Evidence	The New Thought	The New Emotion
I'll never do well in this exam.	Guilt, anger, shame, jealousy.	I have been studying consistently every day.	I will do my best in this exam.	Hope, energy.

THE THOUGHT: THE EMOTION

The table is self-explanatory. In the first column, you describe a negative thought that you are having. In the next one, you talk about the emotions attached to this negative thought. Then, you share the things that you have been doing to discredit this negative thought.

Sometimes, our thoughts have no basis in reality—they are just the product of our insecurities. The *Evidence* column is for any action that challenges this negative thought. The new thought that results are based on this evidence. Finally, the new emotion results from this new thought and makes you realize that *you are good enough.*

Practice mindfulness

Self-judgment, even the subconscious kind where you suddenly end up thinking that you are incapable—can hurt your ability to process things. Mindfulness is important in defeating erroneous self-judgment and replacing it with self-love and compassion. Observe your feelings without labeling them as being positive or negative.

Study the emotion you attach to each feeling and offer no judgment. Instead, just be mindfully aware of the thoughts that give you positive reinforcement, and the ones that don't. You don't need to overthink the connection you feel with any singular thought— because each thought is transient and will pass.

Consciously learn to forgive yourself

When you learn self-forgiveness, it doesn't mean that you are exonerating yourself from the mistakes you make. You are simply giving yourself the compassion you deserve and recognizing that mistakes are natural and make you human.

Giving yourself compassion and acknowledging your humanity are the hallmarks of self-forgiveness, which is not the same as absolving yourself of responsibility or making excuses for what you've done. We all make errors, some of them major. The important thing is

224 | EDRIC SCHUMAN

learning from our errors, making amends if they affect others, and finding ways to get better at what we do.

You are your own work of art. Don't make comparisons

I shared this point before too—so I will just touch upon it. Let others live their lives, and you make the best possible story out of yours. Don't believe what you see on social media platforms—there's always a deeper and sometimes, drastically different story to what you see on photoshopped and highly filtered photos.

You don't get to see the fights, struggles, and frustrations of other people when they only present highly colorized and modified versions of their life. Be real with yourself and measure your progress by seeing how far you have come today, and whether it is in line with your goals and what *you want for yourself.*

Everything aside, *all of us struggle* when it comes to learning from our debacles. It is not uncommon to give up when we feel like we are failing—and it is also not unusual to think that we just aren't good enough.

Whenever these situations arise, I like to use an analogy.

Encouraging yourself through your slips

Have you seen a child learning how to walk? Gosh, do they tumble? They keep falling down, they cry, they scream, but regardless of the drama, *they get back up and try again.* Until one day, they simply stop falling down.

So, upon making a mistake, the winner isn't the one who gives up altogether. The winner gets up and tries again. It's absolutely fine if you get it wrong. Mental toughness mandates that you build enough courage to be willing and committed to the end goal—regardless of the mistakes you make along the way. When the going gets tough, here's how the tough can get going.

- Create a plan for how you want to spend your day. Lay down the main goals that you want to achieve, and leave room for rest periods. Having a plan for the day helps the duties seem less daunting. If you want to use a particular app to keep track of everything, you may leverage your phone's calendar with reminders to tell you when to stop and when to pick back up.
- Make lists and stick to the things you note in them. To keep yourself motivated and get the most out of your workday, begin with the chores you like or are particularly adept at.

Even if your mind isn't in the mood to concentrate, making lists that boost productivity or reduce distractions might assist you in running your day.

- Do everything in small chunks. The more little tasks you can achieve, the simpler it is to stay motivated. Break a big task into small parts and do each of them within a defined time slot. Take breaks between different tasks to ensure you have the same energy throughout.
- Do check-ins. If you begin to feel burnt out or think that if you do one more thing, it'll be a disaster, just pause. Don't force yourself to keep working when you are too tired or too overwhelmed. Take a deep breath, count to ten, and if you think you will do a better job tomorrow, then so be it.
- Eat a balanced diet. Food items that are too rich in refined sugars can give you temporary highs, but once the effect wears off, you can be left with a crash that makes you exhausted. Try to limit your intake of soda, coke, fried food items, and food items that are too concentrated with sugar or preservatives.
- Dress well. Even if the rest of your life is a mess, a good outfit can fix a lot of things. It can also

give a major confidence boost, so try to look your best so that you feel good.

- Finally, audit your progress. Keep a note of the things that you are achieving, what more needs to be done, and how much needs to be completed today. This will help you establish a real idea of what is immediate and what can wait.

We are almost at the end of our journey together. But before we conclude, I'll give you some words of advice to live by.

ALWAYS CELEBRATE YOUR WINS.

The constant worry about what is coming next can deplete you. It can make you feel like you've achieved nothing, and that your life is a constant maze of unco-ordinated actions. Stop. Think of the little things you did today.

- Did you drink a glass of water when you woke up?
- Did you make your bed?
- Did you exercise for 15 minutes?
- Was your breakfast healthy and enjoyable?

- Were you able to spend some time with a loved one?
- Could you begin work on a scheduled deadline?

Each of these things matters. Every tiny step that you take in a positive direction is an indication of you trying to live your best life. That deserves praise—and it merits your recognition. Thomas Edison has gone down in history as the American businessman known for inventing the lightbulb. Did you know that it took him 10,000 failed attempts before he finally found one that lit up (literally) our lives? Well, he had a way of looking at these failures that teaches us that everything has its positive side. He simply believed that he didn't fail, he only found 10,000 different ways that wouldn't work for what he wanted.

To put it another way, he converted his failures into triumphs by focusing on achievement rather than rejection. An attitude of acceptance and a flexible frame of mind helped him to consider even little steps as accomplishments in the direction he wanted.

A key way to do this is by celebrating the small wins. Whenever we think of success, we make the mistake of associating it with only big goals that are most certainly not achievable overnight. The problem with ignoring the small wins is that we end up squelching our motivation—and without motivation, we cannot find the strength to move forward and accomplish the big goals.

Dips in motivation generally rise from feeling insecure about how far off we are from achieving the big goals. Instead, what you can do is celebrate each small goal that you encounter along the way. When we acknowledge our successes, we stimulate our brain's reward circuits and produce hormones that give us a sense of pride and enjoyment, encouraging us to keep going. It brightens your mood and makes you smile.

Stopping to acknowledge and appreciate even the smallest accomplishment, such as completing a 15-minute exercise at 8 a.m., serves as a reminder that you are making progress, which is a nice feeling. Even if you have two hundred other tasks to tackle—you know that you at least don't have 201. That little spark—sometimes that is all you need.

Finally, always try to rinse and repeat your winning cycle, especially within a work environment.

RINSE AND REPEAT THE WINNING CYCLE

The first step to rinsing and repeating the cycle of winning is to keep track of all activities done in your organization the year before. You can make a manual of everything you have achieved. This manual can include simple things like how you prepared for meetings or the big things like what you did to train yourself for year-end evaluations.

Create a system that will enable you to track all your movements so that your decisions are always the output of discipline and conscious action.

If you are the organizational leader, you have to be a model of the behavior you want to inspire in your colleagues and workers. Be abreast of items on the agenda, think of creative means of information delivery, and try to make daily meetings valuable and creative.

Use themes that will get people to put their thinking caps on. Always keep all communication channels open, and ensure that there is enough compassion amongst teammates.

Advise, encourage, and reward your teams if they fulfill the criteria of daily and weekly discipline goals. But don't reward chaos. Look into the source of issues when there are constant delays and try to find solutions that put a stop to these issues. When handling such situations, always empathize with your employees in getting to the root cause of what is going wrong.

While you don't need to reward one person who acted well during the chaos, you can simply share their example and build an expectation of what constitutes model actions during a chaotic time.

With this, we have reached the end of our journey together. Before I conclude, let's just wrap up the key points of this chapter.

CHAPTER SUMMARY

- Learning to forgive yourself is a difficult but worthy feat that makes you mentally tough.
- You should always empathize with yourself and practice compassion.
- Never compare your progress or timeline to that of others.
- Always encourage yourself to do the best you can.
- Celebrate all your small wins.

FINAL WORDS

Dear reader,

You have it in you to live the best version of your life. Mental toughness isn't something that you observe in others with awe and wonder. It is something that is inherently achievable. Each and every one of you possesses the ability to develop and use it to get ahead in life. And, after reading this book, I sincerely hope that you will be encouraged to do so.

Treat this book as a journal of all the things you need to do to become mentally tough. Each skill discussed in the book is not something to be born with, rather, something that is made. You need constant practice, effort, and the willingness to learn from your mistakes.

When you have these three things down, the rest will fall into place.

At the end of the day, everything comes down to routine and habits. We may think that we are independent beings and are capable of making on-the-spot decisions, but even the most skilled improvisers will tell you that they spend hours of everyday learning to improve their skills and get better. Unless you make a habit out of the skills you want to develop, you won't get where you want to go.

Using the strength of habits to achieve success is a terrific strategy. Consistently following a routine helps free up your mind so that it can focus on other tasks, such as decision-making and creative work when you are at your most innovative and concentrated state of mind.

The skills we covered in this book are unbreakability, positivity, commitment, consistency, mindfulness, resourcefulness, and self-forgiveness. Each of these skills can be turned into a habit. Develop them as habits, and you will live the best kind of life. This is my challenge to you. Now that you have the tools at your disposal, it is time to use them.

I wish you the very best in your journey. If you enjoyed coming along this far with me, don't forget to leave a review!

Onwards, now. Make a beautiful life.

You have it in you.

REFERENCES

Bhasin MK, Dusek JA, Chang B-H, Joseph MG, and Denninger JW, et al. (2013). Relaxation Response Induces Temporal Transcriptome Changes in Energy Metabolism, Insulin Secretion and Inflammatory Pathways. PLoS ONE 8(5): e62817.

Block, J.H., & Block, J. (1980). The role of ego-control and ego-resiliency in the organization of behavior. In W.A. Collins (Ed.), Minnesota symposia on child psychology (Vol. 13, pp. 39-101). Hillsdale, NJ: Erlbaum.

Carek, P. J., Laibstain, S. E., & Carek, S. M. (2011). Exercise for the treatment of depression and anxiety. International journal of psychiatry in medicine, 41(1), 15–28. https://doi.org/10.2190/PM.41.1.c

Corley, T. C. (2019). Change Your Habits, Change Your Life. Embassy Books.

Duran, B. (2020). Mental Toughness is Key to Achieving Your Goals . Swim Swam.

Garmezy, N. (1991). Resilience in children's adaptation to negative life events and stressed environments. Pediatric Annals, 20, 459-466.

Greene, R.R. (2003). Resilience theory: Theoretical and professional conceptualizations. Journal of Human Behavior in the Social Environment, 8(4), 75-91.

How to Value Your People as the Most Important Resource. (2022). LSA Global.

Hyperbaric Oxygen Therapy for Adults with Mental Illness: A Review of the Clinical Effectiveness [Internet]. Ottawa (ON): Canadian Agency for Drugs and Technologies in Health; 2014 Aug 27. Available from: https://www.ncbi.nlm.nih.gov/books/NBK253746/

Mandolesi, L., Polverino, A., Montuori, S., Foti, F., Ferraioli, G., Sorrentino, P., & Sorrentino, G. (2018). Effects of Physical Exercise on Cognitive Functioning and Wellbeing: Biological and Psychological Benefits. Frontiers in psychology, 9, 509. https://doi.org/10.3389/fpsyg.2018.00509

Marsh, J., & Suttie, J. (2010). 5 Ways Giving Is Good for You. Greater Good.

McKissen, D. (2019). Jeff Bezos learned these 2 valuable life lessons as a child—on a Texas ranch with his 'Pop.' CNBC.

McSpadden, K. (2015). You Now Have a Shorter Attention Span Than a Goldfish. Time.

Miller, E.D. (2003). Reconceptualizing the role of resilience in coping and therapy. Journal of Loss and Trauma, 8, 239-246.

Mindfulness and Mental Toughness. (2022). Headspace.

Mirza, B. (2019). Toxic Workplace Cultures Hurt Workers and Company Profits. Society for Human Resource Management.

Pappas, S. (2010). Meditation May Boost Mood and Mental Toughness. Live Science.

Piferi, R. L., & Lawler, K. A. (2006). Social support and ambulatory blood pressure: an examination of both receiving and giving. International journal of psychophysiology : official journal of the International Organization of Psychophysiology, 62(2), 328–336. https://doi.org/10.1016/j.ijpsycho.2006.06.002

Steakley, L. (2011). The Science of Willpower. Scope by Stanford Medicine .

Tervooren, T. (2022). The Bill Murray Technique: How To Improvise Through Anything. Riskology.

The Ultimate Guide To Grit, Mental Toughness, & Meditation. (2022). EOC Institute.

Made in the USA
Las Vegas, NV
07 August 2023